PROTESTANT
SPIRITUAL
EXERCISES

PROTESTANT
SPIRITUAL
EXERCISES

THEOLOGY
HISTORY
AND
PRACTICE

Joseph D. Driskill

MOREHOUSE PUBLISHING

Morehouse Publishing
P.O. Box 1321
Harrisburg, PA 17105

Morehouse Publishing is a division of The Morehouse Group.

Cover design by Corey Kent

Library of Congress Cataloging-in-Publication Data

Driskill, Joseph D.
    Protestant spiritual exercises : theology, history, and practice /
Joseph D. Driskill.
        p.   cm.
    Includes bibliographical references.
    ISBN 0-8192-1759-X (paper)
    1. Spirituality—Protestant churches—History of doctrines.
I. Title.
BV4501.2.D688   1999
248'.088'2044—dc21   99-12527
                                                                CIP

Printed in the United States of America

99   00   01   10   9   8   7   6   5   4   3   2   1

*To the people whose stories are
contained herein*

Contents

Acknowledgments   ix

Introduction   xi

1. Theological Affirmations
Introduction   1
The Gifts of the Spirit   3
The Lived Experience of Faith   9
Conclusion   29

2. The Development of the Spiritual Life
Introduction   31
The Spiritual Journey: Faithfulness to the Will of God   32
Beginning the Spiritual Journey   35
A Model for Spiritual Development   37
Using Spiritual Practices   41
Spiritual Discipline   43
Spiritual Direction   44
Spiritual Discernment   45
Spiritual Development   48

3. Guidelines for Using Spiritual Practices
Introduction   53
Skills of the Leader   56
Context   58
The Use of Technological Resources   61
Personal Characteristics of the Participants   63
The Spiritual Practices   67
The Teaching Process   69
Resources for Referral   71
Group Process   73
Spiritual Growth for the Congregation   75

4. Spiritual Practices
Introduction   79
Relaxation Exercises   79
Rule of Life   88
Four-Stranded Garland   92

Prayer of Examen   97
Prayer for a New Earth   102
Morning and Evening Prayer   107
Keeping a Journal   109
Covenant Group   113

Conclusion   117

Appendix   119

Notes   123

Bibliography   127

Acknowledgments

I wish to express my gratitude to a number of people who have contributed to the making of this book. William McKinney, President of Pacific School of Religion, planted the seed by asking if I had developed a book on Protestant spirituality. Professor C. S. Song invited me to provide church leaders from Taiwan with a continuing education session focused on Protestant spiritual exercises. In the midst of this, Debra Farrington, from Morehouse, called to discuss a project on which she was working. When the conversation turned to my work, her interest was piqued and eventually a contract was signed. Debra has been a marvelous mentor through this entire process.

The support of others must also be recognized. I am grateful to the faculty of Pacific School of Religion for providing a supportive academic environment and to the Disciples Seminary Foundation and the Disciples students for encouragement along the way. Mary Donovan Turner and Sharon Thornton have held me accountable to my deadlines and those of my editor. Tim Robinson, my research assistant, has made numerous trips to the library. Jenny Parks has kept me organized. Canines Max and Andy have spent hours in the office watching me type without a single expression of boredom. Through all this Leslie Bryant, my partner, has shared my joys and tolerated my frustrations while contributing to both by making invaluable suggestions as the manuscript emerged. Errors of fact and interpretation are solely my responsibility.

Introduction

Some years ago when I was a campus minister, I was invited to preach at a small rural church a few miles from the city where I lived. A student minister taking classes on the campus where I was serving needed someone to fill the pulpit for him. Acceding willingly to a routine request, I did not anticipate that a person in his congregation would share a story with me, one I have never forgotten.

The sermon that morning attempted to address the way in which God sometimes speaks to us in the quiet of the desert. Using the last several verses from Isaiah 40, I reflected on Isaiah's observation that in the end we will mount up with eagles' wings, but that when things are really difficult we must be satisfied simply to take a step and not faint. I distinctly remember feeling that the sermon had not gone as well as I would have hoped. But my homiletics professor had taught me not to apologize for a sermon, because it was possible, no matter how inadequate it appeared to me, that it might have spoken to someone in the congregation. It was good advice, given what happened that morning.

As I greeted people at the door, I noticed that an older woman lingered to have a word with me. She told me she had a son for whom she continued to care because of his special needs. She said that for twenty-five years she had had to get up every night to look after him. No matter how tired she was, duty required a significant interruption of her night's sleep. She recalled how in the early days she would sometimes sit on the steps to the upstairs to catch her breath after she had tended him. She said it was not long, however, until she discovered that the quiet of her home at two in the morning drew her to prayer. She would sit in the quiet to spend time with God. Over the years these few minutes grew until she found herself praying every night for about a half hour in the hushed stillness of her home. This period of quiet and prayer had become one of the most important times of her day. It was the time she spoke with God and found the strength to carry on with her responsibilities.

I was quite touched by this story. My attempt to address how God may speak to us in the quiet and pain of the desert was suddenly incarnated in her deeply moving witness. With tears welling up in her eyes she added the statement that stopped us both: "I have been praying this way for twenty years and never once have I felt I could tell anyone in this church about this experience. I was afraid they would think I was unbalanced or a Bible thumper if I said anything about it." Then followed her gift to me: "Thank you for coming today. I needed to tell someone in my church about this." Now the tears were welling up in my eyes. On reflection, those tears were not simply tears of gratitude for the gift she had shared with me; they were also tears of sorrow for a church where deep experiences of faith could not be shared without the fear of being judged.

The attitudes and beliefs of this woman's mainline Protestant church shaped not only what she could say about God, but the nature of her relationship with God. For her to experience God's presence in the silence of the night and also speak about the importance of this was to move across the divide that separates evangelical and/or fundamentalist churches from their mainline Protestant counterparts. The fear of being ostracized silenced her voice. Her story reveals the discomfort mainline Protestants have with things identified as "spiritual," for example, a personal relationship with God. It also demonstrates two serious spiritual needs in many churches—the need to nurture an experiential relationship with the holy and the need to recover practices that invite spiritual growth and development.

In mainline churches believers can affirm the existence of God, the importance of the Scriptures, and the need to hear the Word in sermons, but discourse that claims a personal relationship with God at an experiential rather than an intellectual level is largely discouraged. The God of mainline Protestant churches is the "ground of one's being," the God who requires ethical behavior, especially at the social and political levels. However, this God is not a power with whom one would admit to having an experiential relationship. How could the sovereign God of the cosmos truly care about the mundane matters of daily life? Many Protestants find repugnant the joy expressed by those who believe that the acquisition of a parking place results from divine intervention. At a deeper level they are troubled by the intimacy evangelicals appear to have in their personal relationships with God.

The derision mainline Protestants feel about a personal, experiential relationship with God is reflected in their lack of attention to spiritual practices. Prayer, a practice commonly associated with being in relationship with the divine, often remains a child's activity. Children are taught to pray for "mommy and daddy," friends, and pets at bedtime, and to give thanks before meals. These prayers, appropriate for the spiritual nurture of children, do not meet the emotional and social needs of growing adolescents. Yet other forms or types of prayer are seldom taught. Adults fare no better. They replace the "now I lay me down to sleep" prayers of childhood with more altruistic requests couched in more sophisticated language, but the petitionary prayer framework of childhood remains the primary option. Other forms of prayer—such as centering prayer or an examination of conscience—have been virtually unknown to many mainline Protestants.

The disdain for emotive expressions of intimacy with God is also present in many acts of public worship. As evangelical churches offer increasingly lively hours of worship, mainline Protestants exhibit great tenacity in clinging to modes of worship viewed by significant segments of their own members as dry, boring, and irrelevant. Passionate adherence to passionless orders of worship—where oft-used hymn tunes punctuate words, words, words in introits, litanies, and sermons—characterize many mainline Protestant services. Public prayers in free church worship frequently take the form of lengthy pastoral prayers focused solely on verbal content. Times for silence, for quiet meditation or quiet reflection on Scripture readings, are minimal. This lack of vitality in worship is pervasive whether shaped by established liturgies or free church approaches where spontaneity often acquires a patterned uniformity. As a result, people seeking spiritual guidance and growth commonly feel that mainline churches have little to offer either at the personal or the corporate level.

For the last quarter of the twentieth century mainline Protestant churches have witnessed the exodus of those whose religious needs have not been met. The failure of mainline Protestant churches to nurture the spiritual lives of their members reflects a religious ethos that is out of touch with the spiritual needs of many human beings. People who formerly would have participated in mainline congregational life have been looking for other alternatives. New Age spirituality, Jungian psychology, charismatic renewal, eco-feminism, new religious movements, Eastern religions, and Wicca have provided arenas for spiritual exploration and in some cases nurture.

Beginning in the 1960s, there was a breakdown of the appeal of mainline Protestant churches and a turn to other spiritual alternatives that indicated substantial cultural shifts. Since the early days of the Republic in the late eighteenth century, Protestant churches had been at the center of a synthesis between faith and culture.[1] Public life was characterized by a commitment to rationality. The age of science and the age of reason fostered by the Enlightenment had given rise in the United States to a worldview that trusted science and reason. In contrast to fundamentalist religious groups who proclaimed the literal truth of biblical creation stories, mainline Protestants argued in favor of the theory of evolution. The popular movie "Inherit the Wind," which brought together veteran actors Friedrich March and Spencer Tracy, told the story of the Scopes trial in 1925. The song "Give Me That Old-Time Religion" reverberated through the trial of John Scopes, a Tennessee school teacher who had taught his students the theory of evolution. Progressive mainline Protestants identified with the struggles of John Scopes in support of the synthesis they had created between a worldview supported by science and the tenets of faith. The power elites and the great middle class of mainline churches joined on Sunday mornings to worship a God who created the world not in seven days, but through the rational process of evolution.

The 1950s, as it turned out, were the last halcyon days of this synthesis. The worldview that had prevailed since the Enlightenment was disintegrating. Modern physics had discovered two decades earlier that the search for timeless, objective truths was not possible. The very act of observation altered the course of subatomic particles. In the human sciences, theories that gave birth to the sociology of knowledge—for example, Karl Mannheim's *Ideology and Utopia* in 1929—revealed the extent to which human knowledge is socially conditioned. How could one hope to find *the* truth in a world where knowledge itself was contingent on the vantage point of the observer?

Consequently, in the 1960s and 1970s the theological assertions of white, male, European and American theologians were critiqued and found inadequate by women, African Americans, and Latin Americans. If the God of white, Euro-American academic theologians was too distant to be involved in daily life—too high (Karl Barth) or too deep (Paul Tillich)—the God of the disenfranchised of the Third World was present and available in the joys and sorrows of daily life. This theological challenge provided by women and men from other churches and cultures shook the foundations that supported mainline beliefs in the reasonableness of God. If it had been reasonable to assume that God was too preoccupied to get involved in the nitty-gritty of personal relationships with believers, the collapse of the worldview that supported this belief reopened the possibility for developing a personal relationship with God. If groups as diverse as Roman Catholics, evangelicals, and African-Americans could affirm the experiential aspects of a relationship with the holy, many mainline Protestants were now willing to revisit this issue.

At the present time there is neither a theological consensus nor a worldview that binds people of various races, cultures, creeds, classes, and nations together. The absence of consensus produces chaos as well as excitement. Chaos often reigns as old truths are discarded and former authorities are questioned. Yet there is also excitement, for new possibilities can emerge when plurality and ambiguity are the order of the day. In the midst of this turmoil a seemingly intense spiritual yearning has resulted in an unquenchable thirst for reliable tools in the area of spirituality.

Titles at local bookstores across the country have proliferated exponentially. The emergence of this plethora of spiritual materials is both encouraging and frightening. Ten years ago, who would have guessed that Gregorian chant would become a "best seller" in the United States? Would anyone have dreamed that classics from the Middle Ages—for example, the *Cloud of Unknowing* or the works and music of Hildegard of Bingen—would be not only marketable but also profitable? How will these classics be understood by persons who know little of their context? Will uncritical readings of these works bring the meaning for which people are searching?

The consumer society that produces these literary works is also busy merchandising spiritual techniques for a fee. The symbols and signs of things spiritual—for example, the cross—are unabashedly exploited by savvy advertising entrepreneurs. Only three years ago, *Vogue* magazine reported that "spiritual equanimity . . . is only a credit card receipt away."[2]

In the midst of this so-called postmodern time, people need guideposts and tools with which to work their way through the spiritual chaos to a more stable place. Such a place may not be terra firma; rather, it may be more like a lifeboat where shelter from the winds allows the testing and evaluating of the available spiritual alternatives.

There are numerous signs of hope today. Committed leaders remain in mainline Protestant churches even as some of their contemporaries leave. These leaders, both clergy and laity, are searching for spiritually enriching paths that will augment the nurture provided by their own congregations and denominations. During the last two decades, a number of these Protestant leaders have sought renewal and guidance by turning to Roman Catholic retreat houses for spiritual guidance. There they learned their spiritual practices and disciplines that focused on developing an experiential relationship with God. In many instances the religious leadership at these retreat houses provided spiritual direction. Protestants who were recipients of this ministry found that spiritual growth added a depth and richness to life that had been neglected by their churches.

Mainline Protestants have also discovered that they have a spirituality even though they have not recognized it as such. Traditionally, Protestant spirituality has focused on the social needs of the society, deliberately separating prayer from social action. Prayer is often described as a pious, self-absorbing activity and is contrasted with the outward ministry of social action. However, in many Roman Catholic retreat houses Protestants have encountered religious leaders who are committed to both prayer and justice. This stance has provided an infusion of spiritual growth and development that many mainline Protestant leaders have taken back to their congregations.

As these leaders have brought their renewed sense of God's presence to the experience of worship, wonderful things have begun to happen. Today, in a significant number of mainline

churches a sense of God's presence in worship has been rediscovered. These churches are growing. According to Hadaway
and Roozen in *Rerouting the Protestant Mainstream*,[3] this
growth is not dependent on congregational size, denominational heritage, or liturgical style. It is happening in large and
small congregations, in services with formal liturgies and those
with freer forms of worship, and in a variety of mainline denominations. Growth seems to depend on having leaders and
worshipers who are persons of faith who believe that God is
present when the community gathers to offer worship and
praise. When leaders and worshipers believe that God's presence surrounds and infuses them, there is a compelling sense
of the holy that touches the depths of their spiritual yearning.
For those who have discovered that God is present in the midst
of life, the search for a more meaningful and authentic spirituality has not been in vain.

Mainline Protestants are poised to make a contribution to
the spiritual lives of individuals and communities of faith who
take seriously the pluralistic context of the late twentieth century. Mainline Protestants may not know precisely where they
are going, but their contribution comes in part from their
knowledge of where they have been. Commitments to critical
reflection, to hearing the voices of the dispossessed, to inclu-
siveness, and to racial equality position them well for evaluating the marketplace of contemporary expressions of faith.
Mainline Protestants also tend to recognize the limitations of
their knowledge. There is both a critical astuteness and a sense
of humility that allows them to honor the spiritualities of others
while at the same time recognizing that spiritualities must be
subject to critical evaluation.

Yet with all that mainline Protestants can offer, they continue in significant numbers to lack an appreciation for the importance of spiritual nurture per se. If this lack is not addressed,
the contribution of these Christians to debates in the public square
will be irrelevant. If mainline Protestants do not acknowledge
their past blindness in this area and work to understand more
fully humankind's spiritual needs, their other contributions to
the wider religious context may well be overlooked.

An examination of the Protestant heritage reveals that many
of the spiritual practices that leaders and members felt they

had to seek from outside sources were already present within Protestantism. Those who are the inheritors of the Reformation have within their own tradition spiritual practices that are life giving. These spiritual practices provide a number of alternatives for spiritual growth. They honor such Protestant principles as freedom of religious practice, the right to question authority, and the need to balance personal devotion with concern for God's world.

By turning to the Protestant heritage, especially the spiritual life of the early movements and leaders, we discover a spiritual legacy that affirms the Protestant tradition and provides spiritual practices that deepen our faith and our commitments to love and justice. The spiritual practices and disciplines used by the thinkers and doers of the various Protestant traditions fostered an experiential relationship with God (the holy). In many cases, the spiritual practices of Protestants owe much to Roman Catholic prayer practices. Before Martin Luther was a reformer, he was an Augustinian monk who knew intimately the prayer life of that religious community; John Wesley was an avid reader who studied the lives of the early church leaders. Protestants who fail to claim the pre-Reformation church as a significant part of their heritage lose much that is spiritually meaningful.

Developing and nurturing a relationship with God both personally and within a community of faith are essential aspects of being human. Human beings have spiritual needs that transcend the limitations of analysis and reason. Mainline Protestant churches are well positioned to advocate the importance of integrating reason and faith, head and heart, prayer and social action. As we move into the twenty-first century, we are again in a period of cultural and religious diversity, a time during which there is much religious experimentation. The Protestant heritage offers tools that will serve the mainline denominations well as they separate bogus from authentic spiritual practices.

Insofar as an explicit focus on spirituality is a relatively new development in the life of mainline Protestants, it is hoped that this book will provide both congregations and individuals with resources for the journey. The often-unrecognized spiritual gifts of the past are as rich in their contribution to us as the hopes and dreams they engender. Using the lens of spirituality,

Chapter 1 takes a fresh look at five theological affirmations that have contributed to Protestants' self-understanding. These life-giving affirmations give an exciting new depth to our Protestant heritage and contradict those who claim "Protestant spirituality" is an oxymoron! In addition, they undergird the spiritual practices contained in this book and provide the theological context for participating in them. Chapter 2 is intended to help persons who want to incorporate spiritual practices into their daily lives. The focus is on the relationship between spiritual development and personal growth. Chapter 3 describes guidelines for teaching and leading the spiritual practices contained in Chapter 4. These suggestions will aid those providing spiritual leadership by raising issues that should be considered before attempting to lead others. For those with limited experience in teaching spiritual practices, cautions are included.

Chapter 4 of this book is composed of eight spiritual exercises that either emerge from the Protestant tradition or are in harmony with its theological stance. These practices are not attempts to impose outdated and outmoded forms of spiritual development on others in the interest of nostalgia or in the hope of restoring the ancient order. Rather, by reclaiming these practices we can renew an experiential relationship with the divine that offers meaning and hope for contemporary life.

Theological Affirmations

INTRODUCTION

A recent conversation with an evangelical African American colleague of mine alerted me to a freedom most mainline Protestants take for granted—the lack of anxiety about whether they are going to heaven or hell. She said, "It was revolutionary for me as an evangelical to realize that mainline Protestants have not lost a single night's sleep in their entire lives worrying about whether they are going to get into heaven." "Honey," she continued, "that's liberation for an evangelical!" A little further in the conversation she noted, "But I need Jesus. I can't get through a single day without Jesus. You white liberals don't need Jesus like I do . . . to cope with the racism and gender bias that are a part of daily life for me." Then she smiled her infectious, accepting smile and said, "In a way I feel you are missing something. I just have this sense that you all may not have as close an experiential relationship with God as I do. Don't get me wrong, I don't want to be the object of racism or sound presumptuous. But I am grateful that God walks with me each day and keeps me going."

Many mainline Protestants could not speak of God in this way for a number of reasons, among them being the general inability to use theological discourse to describe an experiential or personal relationship with God. As noted in the Introduction to this book, this type of "God talk" has been taboo in many Protestant churches. This discourse is frequently identified with a "me and Jesus" faith paradigm assumed to represent an internally focused concern for individual salvation that ignores social ills and encourages a naive worldview where God's sweetness and light are focused upon, to the exclusion of the hidden, self-serving motivations characteristic of human existence. The ingrained aversion to this kind of "me and Jesus" approach to God has permeated much Protestant congregational life.

As white mainline Protestants increasingly converse with African American Christians in the black church (often in the same denomination), the Caucasians are discovering that having a relationship with Jesus does not necessarily fit the "me and Jesus" stereotype described above. Clearly, the woman who spoke with me—whose relationship with God leads her to work for social justice, to nurture her own growth in faithfulness, and to endure sexism and racism at the hands of others—cannot be described as participating in an experiential relationship with a God interested primarily in personal salvation, sweetness, and light!

As ecumenical and interfaith dialogues increase, many Protestants are discovering that there are a number of ways to speak of an experiential relationship with the Godhead. For example, as noted in this book's Introduction, spiritual directors and retreat leaders in the Roman Catholic Church use theological language to describe an experiential relationship with the sacred. They speak of God, Jesus, or the Holy Spirit in ways that bring theological reflection out of the realm of abstraction and into the arena of daily life. These examples from an African American Protestant woman and the Roman Catholic tradition make it apparent that many religious traditions have kept alive theological reflections and practices that nurture the spiritual life of their members.

Many mainline Protestants are just now becoming aware of what the Roman Catholics call ascetical theology, mystical theology, and spiritual theology. Ascetical theology is concerned with the spiritual practices that deepen our faith; it focuses on spiritual practices and various forms of prayer that deepen our relationship with the sacred. Mystical theology, on the other hand, deals with the fruits of spiritual practices—the nature of the faith development that the ascetical practices make possible. As Christian mystics gain increasing attention today, the works of Ignatius of Loyola are used to teach methods of prayer, self-examination, and spiritual discernment, whereas those of Teresa of Avila and John of the Cross are probed for their insights into the fruits of mystical prayer. These rich theological traditions of the pre-Reformation church, especially as they address issues of spiritual development, are being rediscovered and used today by searching, thoughtful, mainline Protestants.

Although the rubrics of ascetical theology and mystical theology were used more prominently earlier in this century to describe this religious literature, since Vatican II such reflection has generally been encompassed by the category "spiritual theology." This area of study deals not simply with asceticism and mysticism, but with a broader understanding of spirituality that brings it into the purview of all of life.

The lack of attention by mainline Protestants to ascetical, mystical, and spiritual theologies resulted in the loss of contact with spiritual practices, including various forms of prayer and spiritual disciplines. As a result, in recent decades many Protestants found they had no avenue of access that opened believers to an experiential relationship with God. Without the benefit of an experiential relationship with God or the theological reflections that inform and sustain spiritual practices, mainline Protestants have been denied an important source of religious insight. It is these disciplines that can provide an experiential relationship with the sacred and a means for deepening one's faith. By not focusing on these spiritual traditions, or even keeping them alive, the experiences that they provided were also lost.

The current interest in integrating intellectual curiosities with faith-transforming practices is leading mainline Protestants to reexamine their history from the lens provided by spirituality. As these seekers within graduate theological programs explore ascetical and mystical theologies of the Roman Catholic Church, many are being inspired to view their own traditions from this perspective. Consequently, a number of characteristics of mainline Protestant spirituality are emerging that have heretofore not been fully explored, in part because they were not identified as the work of the Spirit. It is important to begin this chapter on theological insights with elements of the mainline Protestant tradition that need to be celebrated as gifts of the Spirit.

THE GIFTS OF THE SPIRIT

The Ethical Conscience

The theological affirmations that inform spiritual practices need to be consonant with the Protestant heritage that has brought many blessings to its communities of faith. At their best, mainline Protestant traditions exercise judicious leadership in the arenas of ethical reflection and social action. Those in positions of church leadership frequently feel a sense of solidarity with victims of oppression and work to rectify social, political, and economic inequities. Women's rights and issues, from ordination to the prevention of physical abuse, have become important on denominational agendas; ministries of social justice and economics both domestically and internationally are supported; issues involving human rights and sexuality—abortion, sexual expression, justice for gays and lesbians—are being debated. Although policies related to social issues do not always receive enthusiastic endorsements from all quarters of the church, attention to them is still a defining characteristic of mainline Protestant traditions.

The ethical conscience, especially as it relates to social concerns, is at the heart of mainline Protestant life. Pastoral theologian Seward Hiltner probably speaks for many mainline Protestants when he says that people come closest to God when they come closest to following their ethical conscience.[1] The identification of "God's voice" with the ethical conscience is a strength of mainline Protestant traditions.

Unfortunately, many Protestants fail to see their ethical commitments to social justice as gracious gifts from God. They affirm that God is a force of love and compassion at work in the world, but inasmuch as love and compassion are not the sole prerogatives of religious folks, mainline Protestants often minimize the extent to which these powers are associated with divine activity. Lacking a propensity for theological interpretation, they view ethical actions in behalf of others not expressly as God's handiwork, but as the work required of any good citizen. By so doing they minimize the theological significance of their ethical conscience and the actions that flow from it.

The commitment to social justice is an inestimable spiritual gift integral to mainline Protestant spirituality. This commitment allows mainline Protestants to affirm that God is at work in the daily lives of people struggling for justice and peace. This recognition has the potential to augment the mainline Protestant tendency to limit God's voice to the ethical conscience. It is an irony that although official Protestant teachings—for example, church doctrines—avoid claims that limit God's sphere of influence, in the "lived experience of faith" of many

Christians, God's leading is largely restricted to two areas—the ethical conscience and the response to profound grief.

During times of crisis, when our radical dependence on God becomes a daily act of faith, mainline Protestants often speak of God's presence with them. The affective depths at which daily life has been impacted legitimizes this often-passing sense of personal relationship with God. Mainline Protestants live their faith in the paradoxical space between being too modest to speak for God except on social issues, and too reasonable to be truly dependent on God except in times of tragedy.

If ethical responsibility at the social level is a spiritual asset of mainline Protestants, it is the complementary development of the personal aspect of a relationship with the sacred—briefly present at a time of crisis—that is required for a more holistic stance to spiritual development. The development of a personal relationship with the sacred may inform the nature of one's social vision and sustain persons who work for social justice. It is the development of this personal relationship that this book addresses by providing a theological grounding and historical background for the practices included in the final chapter. This correcting does not deny the role of God's voice in the ethical conscience. If anything, the ethical conscience is enhanced by acknowledging the links between a prophetic vision and the spiritual practices that keep it alive, vital, and faithful.

Critical Study

Mainline Protestant spirituality has been shaped by a commitment to critical reflection. As noted in this book's Introduction, since the Enlightenment mainline Protestants have been committed both to the worldviews of their surrounding cultures and to the truths of Christian faith. That is to say, as advances were made in science and in the understanding of the workings of the universe, many Christians in Protestant traditions sought to reconcile the truths of faith with the findings of science and the insights of philosophy.

In the sixteenth century Protestants challenged the Roman Catholic Church on matters of doctrine and authority; in the eighteenth century they challenged the worldview that supported the church of the later Middle Ages. The advent of the

Enlightenment established a new standard of truth. No longer was the authority of the church a sufficient standard of truth. Inquiring Protestants adopted a sense of skepticism and doubt toward truths that appeared grounded solely on church traditions and religious authorities. Reason became the celebrated human faculty.

Although by the nineteenth century this commitment to reason did not eliminate a commitment to revelation, it firmly committed mainline Protestant traditions to scholarly inquiry. For Protestants, the question kept arising: How can God's truth be an aspect of both the world of nature and the Word of faith? The truths of faith, the revelation of God in Jesus, and the teachings of the church were submitted to the bar of reason. Biblical texts and historical traditions were subjected to the same scrutiny as so-called secular literary works such as *The Iliad* or a text attributed to Shakespeare.

The biblical scholarship of the late eighteenth and nineteenth centuries easily found its way into the Protestant religious scene of the United States. For example, when the works of German scholars of the Scriptures became known in the United States, mainline Protestant denominations ultimately embraced their analytical approach to the Bible. Harry Emerson Fosdick (1878–1969), minister of Riverside Church in New York City, was a well-known apologist for the scholarly approach to the biblical texts. Critical reflection not only on the biblical texts but also on church dogmas and traditions has been a hallmark of mainline Protestant religious life.

A recovery of the spiritual practices and disciplines advocated in this book does not compromise the mainline Protestant commitment to critical reflection. It does, however, challenge the notion that only analytical—in contrast to devotional—approaches to biblical texts and Christian classics have merit. Devotional practices do not displace critical aspects of faith development; rather, they develop the affective nature of the human capacity for relationship. In addition, devotional practices themselves are always subject to critical reflection; the dialectical process between devotion and critical reflection provides a more holistic approach to spiritual development than either alone.

Foundational Theology

Mainline Protestants are committed to an understanding of God that views all of life as grounded in God's abiding love. As noted by my African American colleague at the beginning of this chapter, mainline Protestants are in general not afraid that God will curse or condemn them. The God who receives their allegiance is the God of the early reformers, the God whose position in the universe is above all human folly and whose message is present in Jesus Christ. As mainline Protestants interpret God's transcendence, they contend that God cares about the big picture, not about the minutia of daily living. The principal concerns of this God have to do with "meaning writ large." The creative and sustaining energy needed to manage the universe leaves this God little time to mess with the trivia of daily life. Karl Barth's focus on God's transcendence—beyond all human manipulation—and Paul Tillich's focus on God's power to ground human existence are concepts that shape and guide the lived experience of faith of many mainline Protestants.

Jesus Christ reveals God's purposes for daily life. The message of this Jesus is primarily one of love, justice, and social obligation. Mainline Protestants often feel that Jesus provided them with all they require for understanding the power of God. This Christ does not require his followers to have a deeply intimate or experiential relationship with him; instead, he came to model authentic living and show humankind the path toward meaning and hope. The ethical model provided by Jesus Christ no doubt contributes to the mainline Protestant identification of the ethical conscience with the voice of God. If God is preoccupied with the big picture, then it is the ethical call of Christ that provides—not a game plan for daily decisions—but a pattern of authentic living. This pattern is expected to inform the daily life situation of the faithful and sustain their spiritual needs.

This focus on God's transcendence and Christ's commitment to justice, peace, and wholeness is a strength of mainline Protestant spiritual traditions. This recognition that the desire to manipulate God—either through official structures or for personal ends—is ubiquitous is an insight that has contributed to Protestants' suspicion of any authority that lacks checks and balances.

Mainline Protestants are especially aware of the way in which statements about the nature of God and claims about "what God wants" can quickly become self-serving and idolatrous on the lips of believers. Because of suspicions regarding authority and idolatry, they have a natural propensity to look behind religious language to see if other human motivations are guiding the religious discourse. Whose needs are being met by claims that God wants this specific action? Does the stated action bring justice or peace for the oppressed, or does it maintain the status quo of the speaker? Who speaks for God? What criteria must be used to discern if the message is of God? Protestants recognize the timeliness of these questions.

Unfortunately, these compelling sensitivities also make many Protestants wary of making any claims about God's activity beyond the most basic and fundamental statements about God's creative, sustaining power and God's self-revelation in Christ. Although mainline Protestant believers are willing to affirm in a general and vague way that God's love creates and ultimately sustains life, they often fear looking for God's activity in the day-to-day activities of living. Addressing this spiritual malaise will require discovering that theological affirmations may address not only these foundational issues of existence but also the issues of daily living. The cutting edge for many mainline Protestants is the recognition that it is possible to maintain one's suspicion of authority and one's fears about speaking for God and still sustain an experiential relationship with God that offers nurture, correction, transformation, and redemption. An engagement with the spiritual practices provided in this book offers an avenue for affirming Protestant suspicions while affirming the meaning that comes from an experiential relationship with the divine.

Although it is probably true that some people are not interested in developing an experiential relationship with the divine, the option for this form of spiritual development should not be anathema to mainline churches. Even for those not interested in further spiritual development, this issue will not simply "go away." The pluralism of the contemporary period precludes that option. As mainline Protestants are in dialogue with African American Christians, Asian Christians, Roman

Catholics, Jews, and Buddhists not only from North America but from other parts of the world, they discover that people from various faith traditions have an intimate, experiential dimension to their faith. Even nontheistic believers often have a deeply affective relationship with the sacredness of the cosmos.

I believe that mainline Protestants can make theological claims that are both consonant with their tradition and that will open them to the affective dimension of an experiential relationship with God without offending their analytical and critical sensibilities. The theological affirmations that follow may seem commonplace, but they provide a starting point for understanding the relevance of theological reflection not only for the ethical demands of daily life, but also for the spiritual growth and development required for finding life's deeper significance and sustaining a prophetic vision.

If mainline Protestant faith is once again to shape the lives of believers in life-giving and powerful ways, the spiritual malaise described above must be addressed. In order to address it, mainline Protestants need to celebrate the spiritual gifts they have received from their Protestant heritage: the mandate for ethical reflection and prophetic social action; the critical and analytical sensibilities that have committed Protestants to an understanding of modern worldviews and the Word of God; and the Protestant commitment to a transcendent God whose mysterious nature makes one suspicious of all authorities who claim to "know God's will" or "speak for God." These attitudes and beliefs are gifts of the Spirit that must be celebrated as well as augmented.

THE LIVED EXPERIENCE OF FAITH

We turn now to the understanding of spirituality that informs this work by noting five theological affirmations that are central to the lived experience of faith of mainline Protestants: (1) creation from breath and dust; (2) creation in the image of God; (3) justification by faith; (4) sanctification; and (5) the reign of God. In each case the theological affirmation is explicated with an eye not only to its intellectual context but also to its experiential potential.

Creation from Breath and Dust

The creation account from the Yahwist tradition in Genesis 2 says that "God formed man from the dust of the ground, and breathed into his nostrils the breath of life" (Gen. 2:7). This combination of dust and breath brings together in the life of humankind the matter and spirit aspects of being human. For the purposes of understanding and using spiritual practices, it is crucial to acknowledge the significance of both matter and spirit in spiritual development.

The contemporary tension in the minds of many Protestants related to the relationship between body and spirit is present as early as the second and third centuries in the works of Christian theologians. Influenced by Greek philosophical categories, these theologians differed in their understanding of how matter and spirit were related to being created in the image of God. For example, Clement of Alexandria (c. 150–c. 215) and Origen (c. 185–c. 254) contended that the image of God is the preexistent Word (the Logos); thus they identified the image of God with humankind's soul and not with matter. Irenaeus (c. 130–c. 200) and Tertullian (c. 160–c. 225), on the other hand, contended that the image of God was the image of the incarnate Son. Because this Son, Jesus Christ, makes the invisible God visible, then both the soul and the body are fundamental aspects of being "created in the image of God." The bodily resurrection of Jesus sanctifies both the matter and the spirit.

The bodily resurrection of Jesus notwithstanding, in mainline Protestant traditions matter has often been understood as inferior to spirit. There is a lingering feeling that even though God loved the world, somehow immaterial aspects of being are more significant than material. Yet the magnificence and beauty of matter as it is manifested in the natural world has always grabbed humankind's attention. For example, the story of Noah and the flood in the Hebrew Scriptures concludes with the divine-human covenant being embodied in the world of matter with a rainbow. The beauty of the rainbow inspires and awes people to this day.

In this book it is essential to recognize that being created from dust and breath involves an understanding of spirituality that embraces an integration of both matter and spirit. In the contemporary context, it is crucial to affirm this commitment to matter as well as spirit because the word *spirituality* is frequently used to reference exclusively matters of the spirit—as if the spirit and the body have little to do with one another. Such approaches use the word *spirituality* to refer to interior acts of devotion, primarily meditation or contemplative prayer. Although prayer and mysticism are certainly important aspects of spirituality for many persons and traditions, they are not the exclusive domain of the term. For example, the last chapter of this book begins with exercises that deal with both body and spirit: the Relaxation Exercise and the Rule of Life.

Within theological education, emerging definitions of spirituality provide understandings that are concerned not simply with interior spiritual matters, but also with the way in which spirituality relates to all of life. As beings of body and spirit, our spirituality must be concerned with prayer and meditation as well as the rich texture of our lives. Sandra Schneiders describes the focus of spirituality for those following Christian traditions as the "lived experience of the Christian life."[2] Spirituality therefore is concerned with all of life as it is lived and experienced by believers: that is, with their beliefs, ethical stands, actions, motivations, historical context, social location, and all other salient influences on the lived experience of faith.

By recognizing that spirituality is concerned with the lived experience of faith, we are acknowledging that one's spiritual life emerges from the complex interaction of the factors noted above. Simply knowing a person or group's belief about a given theological notion does not necessarily shed much insight into their spirituality. For example, numerous denominational groups identifying themselves as Christian could affirm that God is a compassionate judge. It is the way in which the phrase "compassionate judge" informs daily life, however, that reveals the nature of the believer's spirituality. The ethical norms, pastoral counseling paradigms, parenting practices, and financial decisions of a group that focuses on God's compassion may differ markedly from a faith group that finds God's harsh judgment more compelling. Appreciating a person or group's spirituality, therefore, requires understanding the way in which their spirituality is manifested in the lived experience of the Christian life.

As beings created of breath and dust, we belong to communities that participate in shaping our lived experience of faith. These communities provide us a social location that shapes our understanding of reality, meaning, and truth. By exercising an instrumental role in shaping our worldview, these communities both provide opportunities for and set limits on our spiritual growth. For example, mainline Protestant communities of faith, as noted at the beginning of this chapter, are uncomfortable with helping people develop experiential relationships with the sacred. The social location of these faith communities at the center of American cultural life meant that they both mirrored and contributed to what in the 1950s was a common approach to religious faith—one where religious matters were deemed personal and private.[3] With the growth in recent years of the influence of the Religious Right, however, that view is being challenged as we witness the renewed presence of religious discourse in public issues. The social positions advocated and stances presented, however, generally do not reflect the theological beliefs or social positions of mainline Protestants. At the same time, the worldview of mainline Protestants is expanding through interfaith and cross-cultural religious discussions. Both the renewed public religious dialogue from the Religious Right, and the interfaith and cross-cultural religious conversations are helping mainline Protestants grow in areas not permitted by their former worldview.

An aspect of this growth is manifested in the use of spiritual practices that assist in developing both the spirit and the body. Exercises that are used as spiritual disciplines—that is, those repeated in a systematic manner—influence not only the spiritual and emotional life but also the physical. Students of ritual studies note that when the body engages in certain repeated actions, the body itself acquires a memory. Spiritual practices that require bodily activity or receptivity—for example, open hands—create within the body itself (in addition to the mind and spirit) a response that is learned and retained. Dramatic negative examples of the body's memory emerge from stories of physical or sexual abuse where the abused is subjected repeatedly to a predictable and repeated series of actions. In these cases people in therapy frequently are required not only to heal their memories and emotions but also to restore the body memory through therapeutic rituals where warmth and support are provided. The body and its acquired perceptions as well as the spirit are instrumental in influencing spiritual growth and development.

The spiritual practices provided in the last chapter of this book offer the potential for nurturing humankind's spirit, emotions, mind, body, and community. These are spiritual practices that honor our creation from breath and dust. They provide avenues for an experiential relationship with God and locate us in the context of a universe where both matter and spirit are avenues to the divine.

Creation in the Image of God

The notion of being created in the image of God is a doctrine that helps Christians understand their role in the cosmos. This doctrine owes its origin to the story of creation found in Genesis 1:1–2:4a. In Genesis 1:26–27 the writer of the Priestly tradition in Genesis says: "Then God said, 'Let us make humankind in our image, according to our likeness; and let them have dominion over the fish of the sea, and over the birds of the air, and over the cattle, and over all the wild animals of the earth, and over every creeping thing that creeps upon the earth.'" In this passage the words "image" and "likeness" are used to suggest the relationship that exists between human beings and God. That humans are created in the image of God distinguishes them from other creatures. Although this passage has often been used to assert humankind's power over creation— a capacity frequently used to the detriment of this sacred creation—it describes something of the nature of human creation and establishes the bond for an intimate relationship between humankind and all of creation. We are created with a capacity to be in relationship with the creating, sustaining, loving, compassionate power of the universe. Being thus created means that at the most profound level of existence we are not alone; we have the potential to be in a relationship with God.

The capacity for a relationship with God permits us to apprehend the sacred both as the ground of our existence and as it is manifested in daily life. Through our affective life we experience in significant events a depth of existence that is more

profound than the emotions that normally inform our ordinary
experience of life. The joy that seems boundless at the miracle
of the birth of a child, the fragile nature of life that accompa-
nies death or life-threatening illness of significant others, the
overwhelming sense of gratitude that may accompany the spar-
ing of one's life or the life of an intimate are events during
which human beings frequently report an emotional depth that
touches the profundity of life. Persons of faith often identify
this depth of existence with a sense of the sacred, a sense of
being in the presence of God.

Rudolph Otto contended that when we encounter this level
of existence it evokes in us a deep sense of awe, or terror, or
fascination.[4] We human beings, generally at some point quite
early in our lives, are confronted with life's fragile and tran-
sient nature; a relative or friend grows old and dies, a pet is hit
by a car, accident or serious injury befalls someone we know.
When this occurs we begin to ask questions about the nature
of life and our role in the universe. We wonder why accidents
occur and why good people suffer. Tragedy strikes and we are
caught up short, yet we are touched at a depth of being not
thought possible. Sometimes we hurt so deeply we know life
must have meaning.

At other times we are overcome with a sense of awe, with
the wonder of it all. For some, that comes from seeing a night
sky far away from the city lights and being overwhelmed by
the vastness of the universe. Others are awed by the wonders
of travel to other cultures or to alien geological zones where
nature seems unfamiliar. A sense of awe wells up inside; we
may feel both insignificant and graciously blessed at the same
time.

My most recent experience of surprise involving the beauty
of the created world came on a trip to Hawaii. I was visiting
the Big Island of Hawaii, where a volcano constantly sends lava
to the sea in a stream of fire and where waterfalls and tropical
forests abound. Friends insisted that we must include on our
itinerary a snorkeling trip to Kealakakua Bay. Not being afraid
of the water, yet not being an accomplished swimmer, I protested.
I was sure I lacked the skills to manage a mask, breathing tube,
and fins. They persisted, and my spouse, a former lifeguard, gave
me the necessary encouragement to attempt this adventure. I

will never forget the first look I had under the water. My breath was almost taken away, not from inhaling water, but from the sense of wonder and awe. The hues of red and blue coral, the colorful fish of countless patterns and shapes, the blue, clear water—all of this was more grand than I had imagined. The moment came utterly by surprise. With one look through a mask I discovered a world I had never seen—another aspect of God's creativity!

When we are in the presence of such profound forces— forces beyond ourselves—our lives are often transformed or healed. During a small group worship that I was leading, a noted and respected theologian once shared an experience she had had after struggles with infertility. One day while on a holiday in France she found herself watching a relationship between a mother and her young daughter. Her fascination was piqued at first by the laughter and play occurring between them. Suddenly it was as if time stopped, and the deep sense of joy between them became her joy. At that moment all the children on the beach became her children. Although this seemingly timeless moment lasted only a few moments, she recalls that her own issues of infertility acquired a new context, and her anxiety was transformed. She told me that after this experience it would be okay if she never had children.

This encounter with the holy transformed her life. The physiological issues surrounding her infertility had not changed, but her encounter with the holy had transformed her approach to this issue. She continued to go for the medical procedures necessary to enhance her chances for bearing children, but with a realization that if this were not possible she could accept the outcome.

Experiences like this are not unusual. In the 1960s humanistic psychologist Abraham Maslow spoke about peak experiences—those times in human life when we get a glimpse of the divine and a sense that we as human beings are a part of something larger that eludes explanation.[5] We have "aha" experiences that according to Maslow can be small events—for example, a beautiful sunset—or powerful events that lead us to make a major life change or to see the world differently.

For many people encounters with the holy are relatively infrequent. They come "out of the blue" and although profoundly meaningful nevertheless are not repeatable or sustainable. It is as if communication with the profound depth of life occurred, but the likelihood that it might happen again seems relatively rare. Spiritual directors William Barry and William Connolly say these experiences are God's invitations to deepen our relationship with the divine.[6] They claim that every time someone stops to participate in the visual glory of a sunset, that person has been offered an invitation by God to share more deeply in relationship.

Believers following the Christian tradition have the opportunity to relate to God through any of the persons of the Trinity: God, the loving parent; Jesus Christ, the Son; and the Holy Spirit. Mainline Protestants are probably most comfortable with relating to God, the caring and loving parent, or to the Holy Spirit as it is present in the fellowship of the church. But these are only two ways of being in relationship with God. What we do to be disciplined in this relating requires further reflection.

The evangelical friend I mentioned earlier would no doubt say that her primary means of relating to the sacred is through her relationship with Jesus. In her church, people have a sense that Jesus is with them because of his love and their faith. For them, living the sanctified life means having a sense that Jesus is present at each moment. The phrase "thank you, Jesus" is frequently on the lips of some who find Jesus the primary means for relating to God's sacred presence in daily life.

For others, the relationship may come through the sense of the Holy Spirit, either in the community of faith, in small groups of that community, or in a direct relationship of prayer. The late Canadian novelist Robertson Davies, in one of the books of his Deptford Trilogy, has an elderly priest speak about the depth of his relationship with God.[7] This old and now infirm man says that when he was young he never understood how anyone could relate to a ghost, even if it were the Holy Ghost. In his youth, the third person of the Trinity lacked an experiential relevance for him. Now, however, as an old man he greatly appreciates that God is also present to believers as the Holy Spirit. He wonders how, as an old man, he can relate to God through the eyes of Jesus, a young idealist who was primarily concerned with calling people to an ethical lifestyle. As an old man, he experiences deep and abiding relationship with the Holy Spirit.

The deep and abiding relationship with the divine calls us beyond ourselves. It invites us to order our lives in faithfulness to the sacred presence and mystery that surrounds and undergirds us. By moving into relationship with the divine, we move beyond our self-absorbed, self-focused existence. Our life becomes oriented around the values that flow from our religious faith and our religious sensibilities. This form of self-transcendence grounds our life in faithfulness to the divine. As we move increasingly into a deeper relationship with God, we discover afresh God's deepest presence in the midst of our lives. As we have taken up and been caught up in the transforming relationships of those we love, so now we accept God's invitation to be in relationship with the sacred presence that is as close to us as our breath.

The spiritual exercises in the concluding chapter of this book provide a means for accepting God's invitation to love, to work for justice, to be transformed. They acknowledge the God who calls us in the beauty of the sunset, in the last breaths of a loved one dying, in the acts of sacrifice and love that promote justice and yearn for peace. These practices are avenues to the holy for those who will hear either "the still small voice" or the earthquake and the fire.

Justification by Faith

The spiritual practices of mainline Protestants will necessarily begin with the theological assumption that such practices are drawn upon as a response to God's love. They are not used to earn one's salvation. Mainline Protestants have inherited through their denominational traditions a belief in a God of love who offers salvation as a gift for those who believe. This God does not require believers to earn divine favor; instead, divine favor is bestowed on all who have faith. In order to understand the significance of the belief in "justification by faith" for mainline Protestant traditions, it is helpful to review a few formative events at the time of the Reformation and consider their impact on spiritual practices.

Belief in a benevolent God whose grace was freely bestowed was not the norm in popular piety in the centuries immediately preceding the Reformation. The notion of God as a stern judge was common during the High Middle Ages, from the fourteenth century to the period prior to the Reformation. The belief that God delighted in sending recalcitrant sinners to hell kept faithful persons on guard lest they anger this fearful divine power. Many of the faithful lived in fear that they would be severely punished for their infractions.

The Roman Catholic Church claimed the power to mediate God's grace and God's correction to the faithful. The sacrament of penance or confession administered by the church during this period did little to diminish the fear engendered in the faithful. God, the all-powerful judge, could be placated by making one's confession to a priest, receiving absolution from him, and carrying out any assigned penance. Normally the penance imposed by the priest was some act or good work. Confession and absolution were deemed effective only if the penitent had a truly contrite heart.

By the High Middle Ages this process of confession had been complicated by the widespread and increasingly corrupt use of indulgences. In the eleventh century the practice emerged of allowing believers to make a contribution to the church and receive in exchange a paper (indulgence) that could be used to satisfy the penance phase of absolution. The contribution to the church constituted a "good work." Those who could afford it were able to make contributions to Rome and receive indulgences that would meet future penitential obligations required for absolution.

By the sixteenth century, many religious leaders were abusing the use of indulgences. People who could afford them were able to purchase these substitutions for penitential acts in anticipation of sins they would commit. From the perspective of the church, these indulgences had become useful ways to raise funds. But the widespreading selling of indulgences by the Dominican friar Johann Tetzel alarmed and infuriated an Augustinian monk and priest named Martin Luther. Luther discovered that his congregants could purchase in Magdeburg, the region across the river from Saxony, papal-authorized letters of jubilee indulgences (for rebuilding St. Peter's Cathedral) that

Frederick the Elector had refused to sell in Saxony. Luther's parishioners now arrived for confession with these letters that granted pardons not only to them but also to their forebears in purgatory. When Luther refused to grant absolution in cases where there was obviously no genuine repentance, the holders of the indulgences appealed to Tetzel.

Luther's actions created a controversy; Tetzel contended that Luther was failing to obey the pope's instructions. Luther, who protested to Archbishop Albert, did not know that the sale of these indulgences raised money not only for St. Peter's Cathedral in Rome but also for Albert. Albert was using the money to relieve the debt he had incurred gaining papal consent for extending the boundaries of his archbishopric.

Luther's disdain for clerical abuse of indulgences, both in regard to the way they were used by the church for monetary gain and in their impact on the lives of penitents who in some instances did not even feign contrite hearts, created a crisis for Luther. With the publication of the ninety-five theses, *On the Power of Indulgences,* in late October of 1517 Luther's objections were made public. For his refusal to accept the bidding of Rome in these matters, he soon was in open opposition with significant power bases within the church.

In the midst of this turmoil in early 1518, Luther, a scholar of the scriptures, was studying Romans 1:16–17: "For I am not ashamed of the gospel; it is the power of God for salvation to everyone who has faith, to the Jew first and also to the Greek. For in it the righteousness of God is revealed through faith for faith; as it is written, 'The one who is righteous will live by faith.' " Luther had been taught that from God's righteousness comes punishment for the unrighteous. Romans 1:18, for example, contends that God's wrath is revealed from heaven to punish the unrighteous. These passages troubled Luther considerably. "Despite his irreproachable life as a monk, he felt himself a sinner before God and was therefore extremely disturbed in his conscience. He was unable to trust that he could placate God through his own works of satisfaction. He therefore was not able to love God, but rather hated the righteous God who punishes sinners."[8]

Then, although allowing himself to express his rage toward God in the midst of his ongoing study of these passages, he attained a new theological insight. Suddenly he experienced his own sense that one did not have to earn the approval of God, the stern judge. Luther recognized that God's saving love was offered as a gift to believers. His fear—reinforced by the phrase "the righteousness of God"—now was viewed in the context of the earlier phrase, "the power of God for salvation to everyone who has faith." With that change in focus Luther's experience of God and his theology were transformed. Luther no longer believed he had to earn God's favor; it was a gift granted with faith. His earlier preoccupation with moral purity was eclipsed by his experience of God's saving grace. No longer did Luther fear the inscrutable judgment of a severe and demanding God. He knew from his encounter with the text that God's love and acceptance were offered to those who had faith.

Soon Luther's insight captured the minds and hearts of many who had worked to "earn God's favor" by their quest for perfection and by purchasing indulgences (good works). The focus on sanctification, the process of becoming faithful disciples by growing in holiness through prayer and devotion and other good works, was now outweighed by a belief in God's freely given justifying grace. Because God's pardon was extended to those who believed, faithfulness required living a Christian life rather than striving to save one's soul through good works such as acts of devotion and charity.

The focus on justification by faith and the lack of attention to sanctification in mainline Protestant faith communities is a legacy of Luther's experience of God's grace and its doctrinal ramifications for many Protestants, who have been described as being better at "seeking to do God's will" than in "having a relationship with God." The implication is that doing God's will involves living an ethical life. Often this means that one's religious concerns are focused toward the world in acts of justice, kindness, or charity. Mainline Protestants following Luther's focus on justification by faith have assumed that God is less concerned with personal acts of devotion than in living a life informed by virtue. As noted earlier, this has been a mainline Protestant gift of the Spirit.

"Having a relationship with God," although not a focus of mainline Protestant denominations, has been important especially for evangelical Protestant groups. For these groups,

devotional concerns of the heart—having an experiential relationship with God and being faithful in prayer—nourish the
spiritual life of the believer. These issues—often identified
with sanctification—were put on the Protestant agenda by the
Pietists of the seventeenth century. Recovering some of these
concerns will assist mainline Protestant denominations in
their quest to provide their members with spiritual nurture. At
this point it is appropriate to explore an understanding of
sanctification that is compatible with mainline Protestant faith
traditions.

Sanctification

The lived experience of faith in the lives of mainline Protestants
has been grounded in the assurance that God loves humankind
and that ultimately the universe is sustained by a loving God.
As noted by my colleague mentioned in the opening to this
chapter this experience of faith has taken away the fear of hell
and anxiety about the afterlife. If we do not have to actively
worry about salvation because it is a gift of a loving God's response to faith, what need is there for growth in faith? If God
loves us as we are, why do we need to deepen our relationship
with God? Why worry about good works, acts of devotion, or
social concerns, if these are not required for salvation? In
order to address these questions, it is important to understand
the nature of "perfection" or "deepening one's faith" and selected aspects of the Protestant tradition that speak to these
matters.

Working out the dynamic between justification by faith and
sanctification (growth in faith, holiness, or perfection) is an
issue that confronts us now much as it did sixteenth century
Protestant reformers. At the outset it is important to note that
the word *perfection* was used by Paul in the Christian Scriptures. This word, however, does not mean "perfect" in the sense
of being without error. In the New Testament context, it
means "to complete," "to finish." Paul is referring to a growth
in holiness or a growth in our conformity to the will of God
and our relationship with God. Because of the confusion in the
contemporary context, where perfection means to be without
error, I usually refer to a growth in relationship with God or a

deepening of our faith to express the intent of growing in holiness or being perfected.

At the time of the Reformation, the focus of popular piety on acts of devotion and other good works that appalled Luther and many other reformers created a climate for reform that rejected many pious acts and devotional practices as inappropriate attempts to earn salvation. These forms of "works-righteousness" were generally associated by the reformers with schemes for growing in faith or increasing one's holiness. The mystics often spoke of "ladders of perfection" or ascending through the use of spiritual practices toward union with God. Luther's experience of justification through faith created a mood for reform where efforts to become more Godlike seemed to deny the action of God's grace in justification. If God alone saves people of faith out of God's own compassion and mercy, then engaging in acts intended to increase holiness are anathema, especially in a context where such acts have been subject to abuse by church authorities.

The irony here is that Luther was engaged in a form of spiritual practice, some form of *lectio divina*—a devotional reading of the Scriptures—when he experienced God's abiding, forgiving love. He notes that he was meditating day and night when the insight came. This insight did not lead Luther to reject the use of spiritual practices, but it did lead him to reject the notion that spiritual practices contribute to one's salvation. This change in emphasis initiated by Luther meant that sanctification, the process of growing in holiness through acts of devotion, was de-emphasized in the lives of the believers.

Although Luther's doctrine of justification by faith was accepted by most reformers of the sixteenth century as a defining doctrine that distinguished Protestants from Roman Catholics, the emphasis on sanctification varied within Protestantism. In Lutheran groups, sanctification was paid little heed, but in the Reform movement of John Calvin (1509–1564) sanctification once again played a role in the lives of the faithful. Living a holy life became for Calvinists a response to God's gift of salvation. One was called to lead a holy life, not to earn God's favor, but out of gratitude for the gift of faith.

With the rise of Pietism in seventeenth-century Germany, sanctification again took center stage. In 1675 Philipp Spener's publication of *The Pious Desires of the Heart*[9] set the Pietists' agenda by advocating among other things a need for an affective appreciation of the Scriptures and an experiential relationship with God. Pietists believed that the reformers of the sixteenth century had established the governance and doctrinal reforms needed, but that it was left to them to initiate the affective dimension of the reform. The "concerns of the heart" had in their view been neglected by the early reformers. Pietists believed that church members needed to participate in the large weekly gatherings of formal worship, as well as in small groups. Small groups offered the most desirable setting for experiencing in one's heart the work of the Spirit. Prayer, Bible study, and personal sharing in small groups provided the spiritual leaven needed by the larger church.

In the small-group gatherings called conventicles, the work of sanctification was again emphasized. Living a holy life required engaging in spiritual practices that would deepen one's affective relationship with God. Inspired by Johann Arndt (1555–1621), a Protestant interested in the contemplative prayer practices of the Middle Ages, Spener put sanctification on the Protestant agenda. This concern was not intended as a challenge to the widespread Protestant belief in justification by faith, but it sought to reintegrate the interest in growing in holiness that had been an important aspect of being created in the image of God.

In the eighteenth century, John Wesley (1703–1791) furthered the concern with sanctification within the Protestant community. Wesley accepted justification as God's work, but believed human beings had the capacity through their faithful devotions and actions to renew the image of God in which they had been created. The fallen nature of sinful human beings could be addressed. Through a process of regeneration— engaging in acts of prayer, Bible reading, worship, and social action—it was possible to renew within the person the image of God. The church, especially small groups within the church, became the locus of renewal by the Spirit. In Wesley's understanding, perfection does not mean "making no errors or mistakes"; it means being in communion with God and serving one's neighbor. Communion with God and service to neighbor are the marks of being created in God's image.

The Pietists and Wesley bring to Protestant traditions an emphasis on acts of devotion—spiritual practices—including both prayer and social action. Being aware of their concerns reminds contemporary Protestants that spiritual growth and development have not always been neglected or overlooked. Recovering this history allows the balancing of issues raised by both justification by faith and sanctification.

Piety, holiness, and perfection are terms that have been and continue to be uncomfortable to many Protestants. They associate concerns about holiness or perfection with a rigid moral stance, a holier-than-thou approach to life opposed to the tolerance and flexibility that have characterized mainline Protestant church life. The negative valence associated with these terms derives to a considerable extent from the rigid, individualistic moral codes that characterized Protestant church life in the United States during the nineteenth and early twentieth centuries. The avoidance of alcohol, tobacco, card games, and dancing was required if one was to treat one's body as the "temple of God"; that is, to be kept "holy." This concern for personal purity was rejected by many mainline Protestants by the midtwentieth century. Their abhorrence of other denominations who were interested in purity and holiness meant that the understanding of holiness as relationship with God was lost.

In the contemporary context, liberation theologians have addressed the relationship between sanctification and prophetic social action. According to these scholars from the feminist, Third World, and gay and lesbian traditions, sanctification requires critiquing the status quo in order to increase its conformity to the justice of God. Prayer and worship deepen one's relationship with God, provide a vision of justice and peace, and provide the courage and strength to serve in a world requiring radical transformation. Such views contribute to bridging the gap that often exists between prayer and social action.

Both justification by faith and sanctification can be central in the lives of mainline Protestants. Justification by faith tells us that we are forgiven. The notion of sanctification, as Dietrich Bonhoeffer claimed, means that grace is not cheap; it requires the difficult work of growth and transformation. The gift of grace that brings the assurance of forgiveness is the same gift that leads one to respond with gratitude and service. Mainline

Protestants can benefit from more deeply appreciating the experiential aspect of gratitude. Being in relationship with the deeply compassionate and empathic God of the universe contributes to the shaping of visions of justice, compassion, and peace so needed by our hurting world.

The Reign of God

The theological notion of the reign of God offers important insights for shaping an understanding of the role of spiritual practices in mainline Protestant church life in two crucial ways: it establishes the arenas in which God's loving power is at work; and it embodies the grace/work dimension highlighted in the theological understandings of justification by faith and sanctification.

The Greek term *basileia tou theou,* although often translated "kingdom of God," is also suitably translated "reign of God." Reign suggests the dynamic activity of God more fully than the more static notion of a kingdom. This reign of God is the central teaching of Jesus; the term appears more than one hundred fifty times in the Synoptic Gospels. In the Synoptic Gospels Jesus does not explain this term; rather, he allows its meaning to emerge in his parables and sayings.

The reign of God provides a redemption for humankind in the here and now and in the future. Jesus preached that this reign was "at hand." Yet in Jesus' teachings there is also the sense that the reign has a future dimension. A time will come when God's reign will be accomplished. Mainline Protestants have focused on the "now" and "not yet" dynamics of the kingdom. Jesus inaugurated the reign of God, and through the life of the Spirit in the church the reign begins in the present moment when acts of compassion, love, and justice are actualized. Among the numerous scriptural references that describe aspects of the reign, the focus Jesus brought to issues of justice (Matt. 5:20) and social action (Matt. 7:21) in behalf of the disadvantaged (Luke 6:20) have given a scriptural grounding to mainline Protestant concerns for social justice. Yet the reign is also not fully present. The evil and corruption present in the here and now make it transparent that the reign is not fully present. It has a future dimension—a time in the future when it will be fulfilled.

Mainline Protestants have attended to the inherent tension in the notion of the reign of God that parallels the tension between justification by faith and sanctification. The reign of God is given as a gift, yet human beings are also required to be agents of the spreading of the reign. Here we see the aspect of the reign that is given as pure gift and the accompanying need to respond to this gift not with complacency but with faithful, active service. In the parable of the Last Judgment (Matt. 25:31–46) we see the expectation that those who are faithful will tend the needs of the outcasts, the strangers, and the despised.

Because the notion of the reign of God establishes God's involvement with all aspects of life, it is helpful to identify arenas where people should look who are attempting to discern God's activity. The one most commonly identified by mainline Protestants has been at the intrapsychic level. At this level, making time for a relationship with the divine offers the possibility for discerning the way God is at work in one's personal life. Here the possibility for healing, transformation, endurance, support, and change takes place by listening for the presence of God at the deepest core of one's life. In the next chapter I will say more about the implications of this listening for spiritual growth.

Mainline Protestants have often felt that persons especially committed to prayer, meditation, or an experiential relationship with God are self-absorbed and narcissistic. By highlighting the importance of the "social gospel" and the acute need for justice in the contemporary world, some mainline Protestants have summarily dismissed the intrapsychic dimension of spiritual development. This attempt to polarize prayer and social action is most unfortunate.

Some years ago I had the opportunity to take a course that surveyed the spiritual practices of social activists who had made major contributions to their societies. We looked at, among others: John Woolman (1720–1772), a Quaker abolitionist who endured great hardships for his beliefs; the Most Rev. Edward Scott, Primate of the Anglican Church of Canada, whose commitment to justice included challenging dialogues with the business community; Dorothy Day (1897–1980), of the Catholic Worker movement. Those whose lives we examined had discovered the power that comes from integrating spiritual practices with a vision of justice and social transformation. Without exception, the people we studied did not separate their spiritual lives from their prophetic stances and actions. In many instances, those studied testified to the importance of spiritual nurture for keeping their visions and actions alive in the face of overwhelming opposing forces and odds. These were people who struggled to discern the paths of justice, truth, and equity for the societies in which they lived.

People who are engaged in developing their spiritual lives need also to explore how God is at work in their interpersonal lives—their relationships with others. This involves discerning the work of love present in the relationships we have both with intimates and with associates in the workplace. Couples and families often report that, by being attentive as a couple or as a family unit to the presence of the sacred in their lives, they discover a depth to life that would otherwise go unnoticed. It is this depth that has the power to transform difficult relationships and open one to insights and actions that provide healing and growth.

Those who are attentive to the movement of the Spirit may also come to note the presence of grace in social organizations. As articles on spirituality in the workplace proliferate in magazines, many people who formerly thought of spirituality as related only to their inner life or personal relationships now recognize that the workplace may also become a setting deserving of a discerning eye.

Many mainline Protestant churches are exploring the power and significance of spiritual discernment models for managing church life. Although in the past, business models and Robert's Rules of Order have been used extensively, new approaches involve taking time to discern the activity of God in the midst of church meetings and programs. Instead of seeking to control meetings using rules and regulations, the discernment model allows time for sharing as well as time for silent reflection and listening to the Spirit. Mainline congregations are experimenting with taking their belief in the Spirit so seriously that they are willing to listen for the Spirit's guidance. The belief that the Spirit actually is at work where two or three are gathered together now moves from its status as a general theological affirmation without much relevance in daily life, to a belief that guides the institutional life of the church.

For those who are seeking to grow spiritually, the theological belief in the reign of God also reminds us that God cares about the entire world. The planet on which we find ourselves is a gift with which we have been entrusted for our short span of years.

Once we begin to relate to the universe, not as an alien environment to be exploited, but as a sacred order of which we are one small but significant part, the way we live our lives starts to change. If we take seriously our role as stewards, such mundane decisions as deciding whether or not to buy an aerosol spray that destroys the ozone of our planet gain importance. Spiritual practices offer the possibility of deepening the bond we experience not only with God but also with our world. If this bond exists, it is more difficult to exploit the gift we have been given.

Some years ago—in the 1970s—a friend of mine visiting the Grand Teton Park was taking a rafting trip down the Snake River. The naturalist leading the trip was describing the pristine state of the surrounding virgin forests and the wonder of river water yet so pure. There was a sense of awe and reverence in the voice of the naturalist as he spoke of the wonders of nature. Most people on the raft were silent as they apprehended these natural beauties with a sense of awe. All at once one of the persons on the raft said, "Oh, when I look at all those trees I see lots of firewood for my fireplace." The hush that followed that statement was not one of awe! How easily we turn sacred trusts into opportunities for personal gain.

As noted in the section on our creation from dust and breath, the Genesis passage has often been used to justify the exploitation of the creation for human need with little regard for the sacred nature of the creation itself. A crucial aspect of spiritual growth means recognizing the deep connection between human beings and the reign of God. The notion of the reign of God reminds us that humans are merely one aspect of a much larger cosmos.

It is the experiential relationship with God that offers the possibility of deepening the link between human beings and the sacred nature of creation. People who engage in spiritual practices frequently report a new sense of reverence for life.

Although Albert Schweitzer has received acclaim for numerous musical and theological contributions, it is his reverence for life that reflects a deep empathy for the cosmos. Teresa of Avila once said that in an ant she could see the marvels of God. Eyes that see with the perceptions of Teresa and Schweitzer are developed by engaging in spiritual practices and disciplines. These practices deepen our experiential relationship with the sacred and open the way for a more profound connection with the entire cosmos—including the ant. This deeply experienced connection to the universe helps us realize that we rise and fall together; we are one world. It contributes to the shaping of visions of justice and nourishes faithful, prophetic social actions.

The theological notion of the reign of God reminds us that when we are using spiritual practices we must look for God's activity not merely within our intrapsychic lives or our personal lives or even merely in the community of faith, but also in the institutional life of the wider world and in the cosmos. Discernment requires looking for the work of God's love in all of life. Mainline Protestants have long affirmed that the reign of God involves faithful adherence to social transformation. Developing an experiential relationship with the divine offers the potential to locate social actions more fully in the realm of God's activity and to sustain and transform such activity by helping us walk consciously and humbly with our God.

CONCLUSION

In this chapter we first affirmed characteristics of mainline Protestant traditions and then noted specific ways in which they could be enriched: (1) a foundational belief in a loving God who sustains the world can be enriched by an experiential relationship with the divine where God's activity is discerned in daily life; (2) a commitment to social justice can be enriched by using spiritual practices that sustain our faith and inform our prophetic actions; (3) a commitment to critical study of the Bible and historical texts can be enriched by a devotional stance to these same texts.

Several theological affirmations were examined with a view to discovering their significance for spiritual practices that would aid the spiritual growth of mainline Protestants. These theological notions—creation from breath and dust; creation in the image of God; justification by faith; sanctification; the reign of God—provide insights that keep mainline Protestant spiritual practices anchored in the Protestant tradition. Our theological reflections revealed that matter and spirit are not diametrically opposed to each other. Spiritual practices are not intended just for the head or spirit, as if human beings did not have bodies. Also and social action should not be dichotomized. Many of the visionaries of the Christian tradition have been people whose lives embody a commitment to both prayer and social justice. The contemplative, prayerful aspect of life is not divorced from the acts of justice; in fact, it is often the relationship with the divine that empowers social visionaries to take great personal risks in the name of love and justice.

Spiritual practices that will enrich the lives of mainline Protestants must be subjected to the scrutiny of critical reflection. They must not become narcissistic, self-absorbed practices devoid of concern for the outer world. They must recognize that we are creatures created of matter and spirit. They must enrich our faith by moving us toward a deeper relationship with the God who loves us, redeems us, and invites us to be conformed to the divine will.

2

The Development of the
Spiritual Life

The failure of mainline Protestant denominations to nurture the spiritual lives of their members has had a stultifying impact on the spiritual development of those under their care. The spiritual lives of many who grew up in mainline Protestant churches atrophied while they were young. The simple prayers of childhood—helpful and appropriate for children—were expected to meet people's spiritual needs into adulthood. With appropriate nurture, the emotional, physical, and mental characteristics of members matured, yet the prayers of mainline Protestants betrayed a spiritual life fixed at an infantile stage of development.

A statement by second-century theologian Irenaeus of Lyons (c. 130–c. 200), rendered here in inclusive language, reveals something of God's desire for humankind and the profundity of life: God's joy is humankind fully alive. Human beings have been created with such complexity that our minds, bodies, emotions, and spirits form an organic whole. To be fully alive means to honor the complexity of human development by bringing life to each aspect of being human. When one part of ourselves is "out of whack," it often affects other parts of ourselves. For example, when we do not listen to the body's need for rest, we may become ill before we are willing to slow down. When emotionally unsettling events occur—perhaps because of dysfunctional patterns learned in childhood—our bodies often give us many signs. The ache in the head, the pain in the neck muscles, the knot in the stomach, the tension across the chest are frequently the body's method of asking us to attend to our emotional requirements. Unmet spiritual concerns and needs may manifest themselves in a variety of ways at different stages in our lives. Sometimes not attending to spiritual issues will produce physical or mental illness; for example, when life circumstances precipitate a crisis of faith beyond our coping abilities. At other times, extended periods of inattention to the spiritual life may go unnoticed. Ultimately we will be left feeling empty if we do not sufficiently attend to our deepest longings and our deepest, truest selves, the selves we are in relationship with God. This emptiness at the depths of our lives cannot be satisfied either with hectic activity or the latest consumer goods. Only by attending to our various needs, including spiritual needs, can we hope to be "fully alive."

Unfortunately, because many mainline Protestants have not been taught how to nurture or develop their spiritual lives, this highly significant aspect of personal development is found wanting. How can we hope to nurture the spiritual dimension of our existence if we have not been taught how to use spiritual practices as a means of listening for God's leading? We need to be taught to hear God's nudging just as we have been taught to listen to our bodies, minds, and hearts. By learning to listen to our hearts and spirits, we give ourselves the opportunity to face our personal needs, to name the arid places in our lives, and to grow spiritually. By facing the joys and the pains of daily living, we are given the opportunity to choose life, to discover anew that God's joy truly is humankind fully alive.

The good news is that the Protestant tradition itself contains many of the spiritual practices people are seeking. By examining our tradition's spiritual riches as well as those of the pre-Reformation period of church history—which is also our history—we open ourselves to an abundance of spiritual resources. This chapter presents insights into the spiritual journey that will prepare us personally for using the teachings and practices contained in Chapter 4.

The Spiritual Journey: Faithfulness to the Will of God

The apostle Paul asserts that God sent Jesus' spirit into the hearts of human beings in order that they might be conformed to the will of Christ (Gal. 4:6–9). Although such conformity is not easily achieved, it is the life task of Christians to attend carefully in all things to the will of the Spirit (Eph. 4:15; 1 Pet. 1:15). This lifelong need for spiritual growth and development is a continuously open invitation—extended to all who will respond—to embark on a journey led by the Holy Spirit.

Teresa of Avila (1515–1582) uses the metaphor of the castle to help us understand this spiritual journey.[1] She says that a person's soul is like a castle in which there are seven dwellings or mansions. The castle is like a beautiful diamond with the rooms like its facets. At the center of the castle is great light, the divine. The spiritual journey consists of moving from the outer dwellings of the castle toward the center, that is, toward God. In order to move toward the center we must grow in faith by conforming our life to the will of God. As we deepen our relationship with God we move through the dwellings and grow closer to the center.

We must be careful, however, not to construe from Teresa's metaphor of the castle the suggestion that there is only one path to God, or that people's spiritual development occurs in a uniform, linear fashion. Teresa says that there are many rooms in each of the dwellings, which allows for a considerable variety of paths toward the center. According to Teresa, few religious people enter fully into the dwellings nearest the center, but this does not mean that faithful people who live much of their lives in the outer mansions are any less important in the eyes of God than those who more fully give their lives over to God.

An important paradox is present in Teresa's understanding of the spiritual journey. On the one hand, there is a notion of development; the soul matures, and as it grows its prayer is altered and deepened. On the other hand, life in any of the dwellings and the use of any form of prayer is appropriate if it draws one toward God. Ultimately, people are to be judged not on the level or state of mystical prayer achieved, but on their ability to practice the virtues. Throughout her writings Teresa emphasizes the importance of our actions as a means of evaluating our spiritual life. We cannot know what is happening inside people, but we can witness the fruits of their growth. She notes that people cannot claim to be growing spiritually if their actions and deeds do not flow from love and compassion. "If you do not strive for the virtues and practice them, you will always be dwarfs."[2] Teresa recognized the need of this reminder for anyone seeking to grow spiritually as a form of self-centered achievement.

In the cultural climate of the United States there is a focus on individualism (less so in Canada) and human achievement that supports a notion that we must be "the best" in order to truly matter. We see this attitude present in those who want to be "the best" in academics, or have "the best" stock portfolio, or "the best" bottom line in business and industry. It is an attitude that owes its roots to the stories that have shaped the cultural life of the United States—from the courage of the Pilgrims seeking religious freedom to the rugged individualism of the pioneers who crossed the country in covered wagons. In the spiritual life, this desire to be "the best" manifests itself in the lives of those preoccupied with the stage or state of their spiritual development. Knowing that spiritual life involves progress and some discernable markers of growth, these folks constantly strive for the next stage of growth. They worry about their level of spiritual achievement, want to know their developmental stage, and are anxious if they are not making sufficient progress. This understanding of spiritual development reduces the spiritual life to a journey of self-centered achievement.

The goal of the spiritual life is being on the journey. Faithfulness requires trusting that God not only profoundly cares about our lives but also that God is at work in our daily lives. Such trust requires a radical openness and vulnerability to the leading of the Spirit. There is a comforting but also frightening dimension to being in an intimate relationship with the holy: It means that our hopes, dreams, and visions can be challenged and transformed in the encounter. This level of trust moves us away from narcissistic goals and a focus on personal spiritual achievement.

Teresa reminds us that being in a relationship with God requires love, detachment, and humility. Love of God is at the center of a faithful Christian life. Our relationship with God is grounded in our belief that the great, mysterious power of the universe wants to be in a loving relationship with each one of us. God invites us with all of our human frailty and brokenness to reach out in trust. Detachment facilitates this reaching out by freeing us from the demands of personal desires and goals; it allows us to surrender defensive postures that serve to protect personal agendas and deeply held desires. Such detachment allows us to make space in our lives for the movement of God's Spirit within our souls. The attitude of humility allows us to recognize our own limitations and to offer ourselves—with our joys and sorrows, fears and hopes—in prayer. With humility we come to God truly open to the leading of the Spirit.

Such radical faithfulness and openness often leads people down unexpected avenues. I have a friend who had a highly successful career as a high school principal. This person had trained as a biology teacher and had readily worked herself through the administrative ranks of the school system. Through a deep commitment to prayer, she heard the call to leave the comfort of a secure administrative position and radically change her life by directing a social project committed to the needs of young women.

Not all people are called to do something as risky as change their occupations. Some are asked to take strong stands for social justice, in some cases giving their lives for a cause. Others are asked to transform their attitudes, mend a relationship, see the world from a changed perspective. Regardless of how little or how much is asked, the issue is being faithful. Openness to the leading of the Spirit brings with it the assurance of life's most profound foundation, as well as the fear that God may require of us something for which we had not planned.

BEGINNING THE SPIRITUAL JOURNEY

James Finley tells a story that reflects his metaphor for our true and deepest self—the self we are in God. Finley says that for most of us our true self is like having a great house or mansion—a castle, to use the words of Teresa of Avila. This mansion has a vast yard in which is a tent where we actually live. People come along and see this beautiful mansion; we take them up to stand on the porch, saying, "Isn't this great?" Then we walk around the outside and peek up and around to look in the windows. People "ooh" and "aah" and say how tremendous the mansion is. They know enough not to ask if they can go in, and we don't offer. Before saying goodbye we thank them, and if we know them well enough, we admit that unfortunately we don't have the key that allows access. Finley says that we then go back to the tent we have pitched in the front yard, happy to know that the mansion is ours. Yet we have a deep sense of yearning because we haven't yet discovered how to enter it, our deepest selves.[3]

By not devoting more attention to the study and practices of spirituality, I believe that many Protestants have tended to support a form of faith development that keeps our spirituality in the tent. We have not learned—or more appropriately, we have forgotten—how to see God's gifts to us through the lens of spirituality. As a result we have not learned how to nurture and find instilled in our spiritual gifts the sense of mystery and the sacred that deepens and affirms our commitment to the church, the body of Christ.

For many mainline Protestants, developing an experiential relationship with God would require a major conversion. The religious culture of mainline Protestant churches in the 1950s and 1960s was openly hostile to establishing a daily, personal, and intimate relationship with the presence of the holy. One way mainline churches distinguished themselves from their evangelical counterparts during this period was through the avoidance of any religious language that suggested too much familiarity between the human and the divine; for example, phrases like "me and Jesus" or "God told me to do this." Still the longing for spiritual nurture is an essential aspect of human nature, and the efforts of mainline Protestants to fulfill this longing were eventually recognized as insufficient or inadequate. For many mainline Protestants, taking seriously the possibility of having a relationship with God and the possibility of discerning God's activity in their daily lives required a major shift in their approach to God. A new key was needed to open the door of their "interior castle," a key that would allow them to explore their inner selves, to discover the selves they are in God, and to act with compassion and love. That key is prayer.

For some people a new awareness of the spiritual life comes through a particular stance toward prayer, what I call the "technique" approach. This occurs when people attend a workshop or educational event where an especially meaningful spiritual practice is used; for example, a guided meditation, prayer of examen, or body exercise. The positive experience of prayer leads people to search for other events or practices anticipating an equally profound religious experience. Although the technique approach has initially introduced many persons to spiritual practices, the danger is in treating these practices as goods to be consumed rather than as avenues to the sacred. People seeking positive experiences, or spiritual "highs," often move to other practices when the positive outcomes cease.

Using spiritual practices from the Christian tradition or from other faith traditions without an awareness of their theological significance or role in the community of faith promotes the technique approach. This book provides mainline Protestants with the historical and theological background necessary for claiming our spiritual traditions and practices. The practices in Chapter 4 are intended as "keys" for mainline Protestants who want to rediscover the rich resources that are ours to claim.

A MODEL FOR SPIRITUAL DEVELOPMENT[4]

Mainline Protestant denominations need a model for spiritual development that accounts for the variety of ways in which the spiritual needs of their members are awakened. For all its problems, the technique approach does open doors for some people. Others discover spiritual practices through the established programs of churches or religious retreat houses and training centers. Many people also find spiritual opportunities in the midst of life-transforming crises. The following model describes how any of these avenues can open us to our deepest self, the self created in the image of God. It provides insight into the development of the spiritual life as it relates to the interior life by demonstrating the intimate link between our spiritual and psychological selves.

In this model an outer circle represents the external personality, the one people see when they first meet us. Jungian psychologists call this the persona—the part of ourselves that serves as a mask until someone gets to know us well. This is the part of ourselves that wants to put the best face forward. It is composed of the personal qualities considered positive, or "good," by our surrounding culture. Thus we want others to think we are generous, wise, intelligent, warm, caring, responsible, healthy, in control, good-looking, flexible, stable, happy, and loving.

Below this level is another aspect of our being. This is the level most people want to keep hidden. At this level we also know that we are anxious, greedy, jealous, angry, frustrated, vain, unhappy, mean-spirited, rigid, dogmatic, careless, and arrogant. Beneath this level is another level of existence, the most profound. It is the level that represents our creation in the image of God. Here at the center of our being—the center of the castle, if we use Teresa's metaphor—is the presence of God, the Logos, the Word. This inner self, the self we are in God, is continually trying to break out, to inform all of our living. But as long as the hidden level, the level that often makes us ashamed, is kept locked inside of us and is not acknowledged by the conscious part of our personalities, it is especially difficult for the Spirit within to break through. Spiritual growth occurs when we are able to move beyond our outer masks, the persona, to the deeper levels of our being. This requires acknowledging the hidden elements of ourselves of which we are often ashamed. By acknowledging them we recognize the power they have on us, but we also limit that power by bringing it into our conscious awareness. When we do this we free our deeply embedded spiritual core—the image of God in which we were created—to inform more fully our actions in the outer world. Now our actions flow not from a sense of duty and obligation, but from the love and gratitude of our deepest, truest selves.

This model suggests ways in which spiritual growth may occur. The first is with a rupture in the outer world. A crisis occurs that brings a reassessment of life at its most fundamental levels. Separation, divorce, death, serious illness and injury of ourselves or loved ones, financial losses, loss of a job, and the death of a pet are all events that can precipitate a crisis in the lives of individuals. The normal coping systems are taxed, and it becomes impossible to maintain the facade that heretofore has given definition to much of a person's life. When the persona is broken open, the hidden aspects of life begin to pour forth: hurt, anger, pain, vulnerability.

When the persona is broken open, some people seize the opportunity for personal growth and maturation. Confronting the pain is not an easy process; support systems become crucial for successful coping. Ultimately however, when we confront significant aspects of the hidden layer, the deepest part of our being is released and freed to more readily inform life in our outer world. The hope and meaning associated with being created in the image of God bring us into a deeper relationship with the holy and inform not only our hopes and dreams but also our actions. Compassion, fairness, and love become integrated into our daily lives not because they are superficial, culturally acceptable patinas, but because they reflect our deepest commitments and deepest values.

August Meacham, a United Church of Canada minister, told me many years ago that his own spiritual awakening occurred at a point of crisis during World War II. Although I have known Augie for more than twenty years, I knew him for many years before he shared with me the details of that experience. I think his reluctance to share these details earlier addresses the profound level at which he was influenced. I share them now with his permission and largely in his own words:[5]

"On or about September 4, 1944, I was a private soldier trying to break through the Germans' Gothic Line on the coast of the Adriatic Sea, halfway up the Italian mainland. We attacked in the afternoon, and in the attack we came to an open field that our officer suggested we charge across as the enemy machine gunned us from a high cliff. It reminds me of D-Day in France as the Allied troops stormed the beaches. I thought up an ingenious idea and ran where the machine guns were kicking up the dirt. The enemy would then change the machine guns because they felt they weren't hitting me. When they redirected their fire, I redirected my path, and I could run about as fast as a bullet. It actually worked as I followed them rather than them following me. I made it all the way across while others got hit out there in the open." Augie returned to the field under the cover of darkness and rescued one of his pals who had been badly injured. Thinking his day was over, he went to bed in an old house, thankful to have survived. At 11 P.M. he was awakened and told that because he had been there during the daylight hours and knew the cliff area, they wanted him to go back at midnight and participate in another attack. His protests were of no avail.

He continues: "And at midnight I found myself up on the cliff with sixty or eighty men. We undertook to charge the machine gun nests situated in a large stone house. But suddenly we found ourselves in an ambush with guns behind us, and lots in front coming out of the house. At one point I recall watching the waves of Canadians ahead of me being cut down by enemy fire and myself lying in the garden watching the machine guns cutting the corn stalks above me. It was such a confusing situation that I recall thinking that I could not survive. In the light of that, being from a home that did not even say grace at meals, I said a prayer that was awful simple, 'Lord, I'll soon be there.' This was obviously a hastily created prayer. But it totally cleared my mind and I was suddenly at ease and ready to act." The next thing Augie remembered was that all the firing had stopped and he was lying out on the lawn surrounded by dead or wounded soldiers. He decided to play dead with his eyes staring open so that he could see what the enemy soldiers were doing. Their bayonets glistened in the moonlight. When the enemy soldiers were distracted and looked the other way, he squirmed behind a ridge of nearby bushes where a few other Canadians were hiding unhurt. At the request of the Major, Augie, a private, took charge and led the group to safety. He continues: "The simple prayer changed everything. To me, it took care of my survival. It utterly killed my anxiety." The prayer did not eliminate his anxiety forever, but at that moment his crisis broke open his vulnerability, and he opened himself to the presence of the holy.

Augie tells how this experience, far from being a transitory "foxhole" moment of fear, transformed his life. His relationship with God—an experiential relationship—was born. Augie returned from the service to study for a career in ministry. His recognition that in our moments of crisis and vulnerability we may encounter life's deepest, most profound mystery led him on a lifelong spiritual journey. His medals for bravery pale in comparison to the life-transforming depths he experienced in those moments confronting death.

Not all people are capable of using an overwhelming crisis for growth. Some people want to return their persona quickly to its intact state, often by denying the depth of the crisis or tragedy. Those who do this rapidly reconstruct the walls of their personalities and keep in check the power of their hidden, unacceptable needs and longings. When this occurs, a wonderful opportunity for growth has been lost; the hidden aspect of the personality continues to exert its influence at the unconscious level; and the force and integrity of living from the spiritual core is thwarted or truncated.

Accessing our spiritual core, however, is not dependent solely upon a positive response to personal crisis. Another meaningful avenue for growth occurs when we engage in spiritual exercises, including prayer practices. These practices have the potential to make the structures of our conscious life more flexible. That is, spiritual practices serve as a container for the hidden, unconscious material and permit aspects of the hidden layer of our personalities to flow into conscious life at what for most people is a manageable pace. Instead of the hidden layer with its fears, pains, and frustrations rushing out—as usually happens in a crisis—this hidden material eases out as we also access the goodness and graciousness of our spiritual core. In either case, however, whether spiritual development occurs as a result of crisis, or more slowly through regular practices and prayer, spiritual and emotional development are intertwined throughout our spiritual journey.

USING SPIRITUAL PRACTICES

Because spiritual and emotional development are so intertwined, it is useful to understand how our emotional temperaments and preferences may influence our spiritual practices. In the beginning stages of spiritual growth, finding exercises that are compatible with our personal style may be crucial. People who are highly extroverted often tell me the last thing that would attract them to spiritual practices is spending a large chunk of time in silence each day. For these people a practice that involves action or the use of the imagination—for example, walking devotionally or using a guided image—might be a more appropriate starting point. For those who seek quiet and need time for personal reflection, practices that involve silence—for example, centering prayer—might be a helpful place to begin. There are many ways to nurture the spirit and become more fully conscious of the working of the Holy Spirit in our lives.

Building on things we already do to nurture the spirit—even if we have not thought of them as spiritual practices—gives us a sense of things compatible with our emotional temperament. The Rule of Life practice in Chapter 4 will be a helpful starting place for many.

A more structured means of linking our spiritual practices to our individual temperaments or personality preferences would involve using either the Myers-Briggs Personality Type Indicator or the Enneagram to gain insight into our psychological preferences. Much literature has been written about spiritual practices from the perspective of these personality tools. Beginners may use these personality tools to highlight and follow the spiritual practices most closely associated with their personality types, whereas more experienced people may seek spiritual growth by using practices that challenge or stretch their preferences. Spiritual directors may be helpful in teaching directees to maximize the use of these tools.

Beginners need to give themselves permission to experiment with a variety of spiritual practices. The delicate balance involves experimenting enough to discover a practice that is helpful, without getting caught by the temptation to jump from one exercise to another without knowing enough about any of them to discover their usefulness. Spiritual practices have an integrity that is discovered only when they are used in a prayerful, sustained manner.

When used consistently, spiritual practices open us to the presence of the holy in our midst. Although as Protestants we affirm that God's mercy is a gift that is freely given, we also know that as human beings we are called to be in relationship with God. Being in a relationship with the divine mystery that sustains and transforms our very existence requires something of us. It requires among other things honesty, love, support, openness, vulnerability, forgiveness, and trust.

Spiritual practices provide the framework for our relationship with God. The Spirit cannot be manipulated. We do not engage in spiritual practices as a means of forcing God's self-revelation. Those who encounter the holy while using a spiritual practice sometimes believe that if they engage in the practice again God will be there in exactly the same way. People more experienced with spiritual practices understand that being in a relationship with God is not unlike being in a relationship with another person. Sometimes the person is present to us as we anticipate and sometimes not. We come to the relationship with God saying, "This is where I am," "This is how things are right now," or we come simply in the quietness of our hearts. We make time for God, not knowing how or where God may be leading us at any particular time. Waiting for God in the quietness of prayer, on a walk through the woods, or while marching for peace involves opening ourselves to the Spirit, knowing that God responds not always according to our wishes but according to our needs.

SPIRITUAL DISCIPLINE

Spiritual practices are most helpful when they are integrated into the fabric of our daily lives. Using them in a disciplined manner over time increases our awareness of the holy. The notion of discipline is pivotal. Some people shy away from this word because they associate it with severe parental punishment or rigid adherence to a meaningless practice. For them the routine repetition of an activity has a life-draining rather than life-sustaining character. Discipline in its Latin derivation, however, refers to "instruction" or "learning." It is through discipline that we learn how to develop our skills; for example, playing the piano or nurturing a relationship. Learning a spiritual practice has some things in common with learning a second language. Language acquisition does not occur unless one engages in the discipline of daily study and practice. In contrast to other forms of subject matter, attempting to cram a few hours before a language exam usually yields little benefit. Developing a relationship with God requires attending to the relationship each day. One cannot "cram" with spiritual exercises, hoping that the relationship with the holy will suddenly mature. Spiritual exercises structure our relationship with God and are of most value when used on a regular basis.

The sacred only occasionally breaks into our lives in highly unanticipated ways through unusual means. More often, regularly engaging in a meaningful spiritual practice is the path required for learning how to relate to the holy. Developing a relationship with the Spirit involves many hours of faithfulness even when it may appear that nothing at all is happening. Sometimes people using spiritual disciplines report that their prayer life seems stagnant or dry, while noting that other dimensions of their lives seem to have a joy or profundity they had not before noticed. Beginners may not realize that even when prayer seems dry it may be enriching other aspects of our lives. Identifying the presence of the holy is not always a self-evident task. Guidance in using spiritual exercises to deepen our awareness of God can be indispensable for those intent on exploring the spiritual life.

SPIRITUAL DIRECTION

Spiritual direction is the guidance provided by an individual or small group to people desiring to deepen their spiritual lives. In the Roman Catholic tradition, spiritual direction usually refers to a one-on-one relationship with a person with experience on the spiritual journey who provides feedback and support for someone less experienced. Both people recognize that in the context of direction they are seeking to discover more fully ways in which God is present in the life of the directee. In this sense God is recognized as the director of both parties, although the focus is on the life of the directee.

In mainline Protestant traditions it is less likely that people will have individual directors. Although it is increasingly common for Protestant clergy to seek out individual direction, it is not expected of them as it often is for Roman Catholic leaders. For many mainline Protestant church members, spiritual direction is most likely to occur in small groups. These groups may be church programs—for example, a four- or six-week group committed to spiritual growth—or *ad hoc* groups of friends or associates who provide peer-group support and guidance. Those who are consciously striving to develop themselves spiritually by using spiritual practices are well advised to have a forum for discussing their spiritual growth.

Spiritual direction, whether from an individual or in a small-group context, provides a setting for the intimate sharing of one's inner journey. At times this material may be difficult to sort out, and the support and guidance of a spiritual director is essential. As human beings we have a great capacity to sense that God is leading us down paths that, in reality are more self-serving than faithful. People with relationships in turmoil, for example, may seek to escape the situation to avoid their own pain rather than respect the needs of others and negotiate with integrity. Careful observers are able to raise key questions and share observations that help us look carefully before assuming that our interpretation of God's desire for us is accurate. Engaging in this sharing while intentionally in the presence of God (for example, represented by an empty chair or a burning candle) provides an opportunity to test one's journey with a representative of the wider faith community. Receiving spiritual guidance while on the journey is an invaluable resource for faithful and healthy spiritual development.

Some people discover through consultation with a spiritual director that God is leading them to face past, yet unresolved, emotional traumas. In some instances, coping with highly significant affective material requires the support of other health-care professionals; for example, trained pastoral counselors, psychiatric social workers, psychologists, or psychiatrists. Spiritual directors are often helpful when a referral is desirable, because they frequently know other professionals who value the spiritual life. Spiritual directors who make referrals sometimes continue to meet with the directee to reflect on God's ongoing leading.

SPIRITUAL DISCERNMENT

For many of us, God's leading is often quiet and step-by-step. As mainline Protestants, we often assume that God's leading is so unobtrusive that we push ahead doing what we think is right without attending to God's presence in the mundane activities of daily life. Learning to examine our routine activities with an eye toward the work of the Spirit deepens our faith and draws us more closely into a relationship with the holy.

Where do we look for the movement of divine compassion and justice? Exploring four specific areas of our lives starts us on the journey: the intrapersonal (How is God leading and transforming my inner life?), the interpersonal (Where is God at work in my personal relationships?), the structural (Where is God at work in institutions?), and the environmental (Where is God leading in the realm of nature?).[6] God's activity, of course, is not always so discrete as these four categories suggest, and in many instances God's leading at one level has an impact on other levels. For instance, in prayer you could receive the courage (intrapersonal level) required to correct an injustice in your workplace (structural level).

Only recently have church governance models (structural level) included periods of prayer and reflection in the midst of decision making. Robert's Rules of Order, a system of organizational maneuvers designed to maintain the control of the chair in structured discussions, is often the primary procedure used in church business meetings. Providing quiet spaces for reflection on the movement of the Spirit during decision-making processes is quite new to many parishes. Although most church meetings begin and close with prayer, few actually listen for the Spirit during times of deliberation. Allowing participants to focus on God's leading in our organizational lives might have surprising consequences. Mundane decisions could acquire spiritual significance. For example, a few years ago I participated in a middle-level judicatory that met monthly on Tuesdays in the early afternoon. The time of the meeting insured that persons in the workforce and young people, many of whom were students, could not attend. Clergy and retired people controlled the organization. The suggestion was made to change the meeting time. Immediately many people spoke of the personal convenience of the established time. Then someone said, "What do you think God wants for this gathering? Is there a chance God might want us to be more inclusive and hold these meetings when young people and those in the workforce could participate?" The silence that followed was unplanned but poignant. When the vote was taken, there was agreement that an evening time should be instituted for a six-month trial period. Making the decision on the basis of our theological commitments rather than our personal convenience brought a willingness to be open to new possibilities.

Six months later the decision was evaluated. The data indicated that overall attendance had increased and that representation from the young and middle-aged segments of the membership was up. There had been a slight decline in participation by retired persons. Debate concluded after someone explained that a retired person not present was unable to attend evening meetings. The vote was called with no mention of what best served the mission of the church. By a slim majority, the meeting was returned to its traditional early afternoon time. I wonder if people again had been asked to reflect on God's wishes for the church if the new meeting time would have been sustained. Often we vote not on the basis of our understanding of how God's Spirit may be at work in our organizational life, but on the basis of our personal needs and wishes. Attention to the various areas where God works in our lives offers us the possibility not only to see a new heaven and a new earth, but also to see how voting on a mundane decision can be a matter of faithfulness.

Spiritual discernment requires examining our daily lives using both our heads and our hearts. Jonathan Edwards (1703–1758), a Congregational minister from New England, in his book *A Treatise Concerning Religious Affections* notes that an experiential relationship with God requires paying attention to the affective dimension of the heart while not surrendering the capacity for reason. Living during a time of great religious revival, Edwards celebrated religious experiences, describing one of his own encounters with God as "inward, pure, [and] soul animating." He also knew that emotional responses need to be subjected to the bar of discernment. People who have active imaginations can easily become so engrossed in their personal experiences that they fail to consider that their experiences may not be from God. Not all affective experiences come from God, and not all of God's activities in our lives require dramatic emotional accompaniments.

Although some people report the occurrence of mystical visions and sudden life-transforming events when being led by the Spirit, the presence of humility is the more common sign of God's leading. According to Edwards, this sense of humility emerges not from the will, but from the heart. It does not grow from a sense of one's responsibility to be humble (a more intellectual process), but from a profound, deeply experienced sense of humility. When God is at work in our lives, this spirit of meekness and quietness can nevertheless give people the courage to take bold actions. Ultimately, God's movement brings forth the desire to love and serve others. Acts of justice, service, and compassion in life's various arenas are the fruits of the Spirit. In the last analysis they are the only sure signs we have that we are being led by the Holy Spirit.

SPIRITUAL DEVELOPMENT

With practice and guidance we become more attuned to God's leading, we deepen our relationship with God, and we increase our sense of the holy in all of life. Over time these small incremental movements of the Spirit have the capacity to transform our perceptions of the world. For example, an inclusive language rendering of Jonathan Edwards' response to the environment reflects this development: "God's excellency and wisdom, purity and love, seemed to appear in every thing; in the sun, moon, and stars; in the clouds, and blue sky; in the grass, flowers, trees; in the water and all nature; which used greatly to fix my mind."[7] Many people report that by deepening their relationship with God over months and years they notice significant changes in their lives: personal attitudes are transformed, troublesome relationships may be understood in new ways, even healed, or institutional responsibilities may demand an increased level of moral accountability. The changes that come when we attend more fully to God's leading constitute spiritual development. In response to our ongoing faithfulness, our fundamental relationship with the world shifts in small but perceptible ways.

Much that is written about the spiritual life identifies exercises that facilitate spiritual development. Learning to surrender, to let go of things we hold tightly, enables us to engage in the self-sacrifices that may be demanded of us; for example, giving up an object we desire, or a dream, or a hope. Here the emphasis is on giving God control of our lives and being willing to turn over to God the use of our gifts and talents. Spiritual practices that require us to "let go" and "give away" are especially helpful for those who have gifts and talents that God may want to use in unanticipated ways or for those who because of infirmity or age must "let go" of their former talents and activities. In either case, the people learning to surrender are giving up something that has been an important aspect of their daily life.

In our early years, God is working to build within us things that give meaning and significance to life. Such growth involves not only developing a strong sense of self, but a self that has something to contribute to others. During the years of youth and young adulthood, our religious focus is often on matters of ethics. As personal character is developed, learning the significance of our own value system—not simply as a set of ethical standards but as a way of life—involves the confirmation that life experience provides. Here the spiritual task involves discovering the benefits and satisfactions that come from living with deeply held convictions inspired by our religious devotion. Life experience—mistakes that come with missing the mark and some outright failures—open most people to deeper levels of compassion and forgiveness.

We know that the maturation process involves not only spiritual growth, but identifiable stages of cognitive, moral, and faith development.[8] Gender research has identified ways in which these developmental processes differ for women and men.[9] For example, at the time of adolescence women are often expected to suppress their dreams, wishes, and goals, and defer to those of their male counterparts. This socialization may be inadvertently supported if young people, especially young women, are taught spiritual exercises that focus almost exclusively on surrender and "letting go."

Spiritual exercises helpful to people in the first half of life build the sense that God is present in hopes and dreams, compassion and forgiveness, fresh starts and avenues of service. Here the focus may be on co-creation and co-operation rather than on surrender and sacrifice. An overemphasis on the sin of pride or the virtue of humility with those in the first half of life may be misplaced. God does not ask people to give away or let go of things that they may not yet possess. Thus, for younger people appropriate spiritual exercises involve claiming God's presence and gifts.

For many people after midlife (between thirty-five and fifty) religious convictions become less a matter of correct behavior than of ultimately trusting the God of the cosmos. The focus of faith shifts from a God who monitors correct behavior to a God who loves and blesses all creation. This is the God we come to trust, to know as the one who sustains, transforms, and leads us even in the face of life's suffering and evil. This is the God we trust at the deepest core of our being; the one whose presence is there even in the midst of injustice, suffering, and death. This is the God who leads us to work for justice and peace—not because we fear a morally upright God who condemns us when we err—but because the Holy Spirit within us longs for a just and equitable world. This is the level of trust that Martin Luther experienced when he suddenly recognized that it is our faith that saves us, not our achievements. It is our faith, our trust, our willingness to embrace the sacred mystery with its unfathomable paradoxes of dust and breath, joy and sorrow, life and death, that gives life its meaning.

In the later years of life, our spiritual journey opens to us the possibility of deepening our trust until we can surrender even ourselves. Thus, for persons in the second half of life, exercises that explore the delight that can come through surrender may be more meaningful. Teresa describes this surrender as the time of blessed union with the divine light at the core of our being. It is known most completely to but a few. Most of us are not called to this level of union with God until our own deaths. But those who have experienced this union—even fleetingly—point the way for us. They remind us that ultimately things are in God's hands, not ours. In human terms, nothing counts and everything counts. Even the most holy person remains faithful only in little ways. Such devotion is recognized as of the Spirit not because of our position in life, holy state, ecstatic experiences, or miraculous visions, but by the fruits of our lives. Such fruits—acts of compassion and justice—are carried out not for merit, but out of gratitude for the gift of love. Faithfulness is the goal. Such faithfulness requires being on a journey guided by a mysterious God who loves us just as we are, yet who calls us to astonish even ourselves.

In the final analysis, we must remember that although we do our part to further our spiritual development, ultimately all of life is under God's guidance. As a reminder of this, I have always enjoyed the story of the old, uneducated hermit who lived on an island a few miles from the mainland. A righteous and caring group of monks who lived in a religious community on the mainland were encouraged to undertake, as an aspect of their mission, the spiritual training of this poor old hermit.

One day the abbot directed his men to set out by boat and spend a day teaching the old hermit insights into the spiritual life. The young men believed one day of training would not permit much growth in such an old man, especially if one subtracted the rowing time to reach and return from the island. Nevertheless they set out as directed. When they reached the island, the old hermit was at the shore with a smile and a word of greeting. He offered them what hospitality he could—simple though it was—and graciously spent the day being tutored by these helpful but mildly condescending young men. As sunset approached, the young monks returned to their boat satisfied that they had taught the older fellow ten rules for developing his spiritual life. Tired after a full day of teaching, they began to row back toward the mainline. You can imagine their surprise when a few minutes later the old man came running across the water toward their boat shouting, "Remind me again. What was rule number nine?"

Hospitality, humility, quietness of spirit, moral courage, and walking with God are gifts freely bestowed by the Spirit. Formal training, wise directors, and loving communities of faith help us along the path, but ultimately God is the guide for us all. This God who guides us enjoys surprises and has a better sense of humor than most of us can even imagine!

3

Guidelines for Using
Spiritual Practices

INTRODUCTION

Darkness was descending; in the distance lightning was streak-
ing across the night sky as the campers and their counselors
made their way into the hills. Emotions were running high,
for this was the last night of a week-long camp experience for
senior teens. Friendships and intimate relationships had been
established among people who likely would not see each other
again until camp time next summer. The closing service of communion held each year in these hills was the spiritual apex of
the week for campers and counselors alike.

The storm seemed far off. Counselors assured the campers
there would be plenty of time for the service and for the modest
hike back to the center of the campgrounds before any serious
storm materialized. Perhaps the flashes in the sky were "heat"
lightning, in which case there would be no storm at all.

Darkness would descend by the time people communed,
even though it was near the time of the summer solstice. The
fading light was augmented by candles on the holy table and
in the hands of communicants. Campers were invited to come
forward in twos to kneel and receive the sacrament. If you were
lucky, you got to kneel with that someone special—that person
you feared you might not see again for another year.

On this particular occasion the distant storm moved much
more quickly than anticipated. As the last dozen campers
waited to kneel by the table, small drops of rain started to fall.
The distant ominous clouds quickly moved overhead, bringing
with them pitchforks of brilliance. The God of childhood, whose
bowling caused the thunder, was on this occasion hitting one
strike after another! Those who had taken communion were
encouraged not to stay for the last song, but to head directly
back along the trail—back up and over those hills—to camp-
ground central. The counselors who were presiding at the table
had their fingers crossed behind their backs as they tried to
distribute the elements to the last of the campers. Could they

finish and make it back to cover before the downpour? Tension
was present on the faces of senior staff members, who were
trying to decide if they should abandon the service and complete it in the less compelling setting of the camp mess hall.
Would the campers be disappointed if they did this? Those who
wanted to finish the service outside prevailed even though the
thunder was intense. As the last of the communicants left the
kneeling bench, they ran for shelter with sheets of rain nipping
at their heels.

In the midst of this emotional, spiritual, and environmental
turmoil, friends were worried about friends—the ones they hoped
to kneel with and the others. Those who communed first worried that others left behind would be hit by lightning—not an
altogether unrealistic worry in that part of the country. Others
were disappointed that this peak experience in the week had
gone from just the right amount of darkness, wind, and cloud—
the kind that fosters a sense of mystery—to a rather anxious,
even frightening, time.

As the folks near the end of the line came running through
the mud to safety, one of the earlier communicants sat sobbing
at a table outside the mess hall. These were not ordinary tears;
the accompanying hysteria made it easy to determine that this
was the sobbing of perhaps a psychotic break or, if not that,
some other emotional disturbance that would require immediate medical attention. By design, the camp was in the country, many miles from even a general practitioner. The wait for
assistance would be long. The distressed person was quickly
escorted to a nearby cabin for the wait.

Given the lateness of the hour, the rest of the campers were
sent to their cabins for the night. As soon as the "lights out"
time arrived, however, the sounds of sobbing became ubiquitous.
Other campers, anxious and stressed with the events of the late
evening, now began to panic and cry. The counselors soon
recognized they had a campwide problem with which to deal.
Within a few minutes all the campers were brought together in
the large recreation hall. As cabin after cabin of male and fe-
male campers arrived at the recreation hall in some version of
their sleepwear, "lights out" became an unanticipated opportunity to play a game of Ping-Pong or floor ball. The emotional
climate had moved from the "spell" of communion, to the fear

of the storm, to the panic at the sight of an emotional breakdown, to the realization that a companion was so seriously dis-
traught. Games, food, and a reassuring explanation from the
camp director made it possible for folks to return later to their
cabins to sleep on this last night of camp.

Factual and apocryphal stories of the escapades of camp
abound. Those who have been present on occasions where
things have "gone wrong," however, have learned that being
prepared means much more than simply reading the material
one plans to teach. In the case noted above, could the anxious
moments have been prevented? Perhaps, perhaps not. But decisions that were made to promote an emotional experience of
communion received considerable assistance that evening from
the natural world. Underestimating the potential for a major
electrical storm contributed enough emotion to an already
charged atmosphere to push some adolescents over the edge.
What might have been a warm and intimate experience of solidarity and thanksgiving at the communion table quickly became a scene of anxiety and fright. Attention to factors such
as context, age of the participants, the nature of the practice
(in this case, the celebration of the Eucharist), and the needs
of the participants might have altered the outcome.

Leaders who use spiritual exercises, practices, and rituals
need to recognize that they are in the presence of symbols and
narratives that hold considerable emotional and spiritual power
in the lives of believers. Approaching these practices with a
sense of the holy as well as with care and wisdom will minimize the probability that a scene like the one just described
will occur. If it does—and we cannot prevent all unforeseen
eventualities—we can be prepared to take appropriate action.
In this chapter we will look at some of the cautions and per-
missions needed for leading groups in spiritual practices.

Many mainline Protestants first discovered spiritual exercises and practices through what I call the "technique method."
By this I mean that someone experiences a new insight or experience of the sacred by using a spiritual practice, and they
want to "try it again." For example, a Bible passage comes alive
through the use of a spiritual exercise, or a new style of prayer
suddenly touches someone deeply, and remarkably it seems that
the Holy Spirit is available at our beck and call. Sometimes

people who have had a positive experience are eager to teach others in their Bible study or church-school class. The assumption is that others will have a similar positive experience. The practice that has so profoundly influenced their lives is treated as a newly found technique that *must* be shared with others. This pathway to spiritual practice may well open a door to the Spirit. However, when spiritual practices are taken out of context and used as techniques their use brings some risks. Conscientious leaders will want to explore more deeply the theological significance of the practice, the tradition to which it belongs, and how to use it responsibly.

In this section we will look at guidelines useful for those who are asked to teach spiritual practices to others. Some suggestions are directed to trained religious professionals; others are intended for lay leaders who feel a call to lead spiritual practices. The section is not comprehensive; it raises cautions and concerns that relate specifically to the teaching of spiritual practice. It offers suggestions for using spiritual practices that respect their power to heal and their potential to harm (when used improperly). In the litigious society in which we live, people are being sued for malfeasance at alarming rates. Can you imagine being sued for teaching someone to pray! Yet the power of prayer to open us to God's presence and to open us to material that we may have repressed cannot be denied. It is advisable for those who use spiritual practices to be aware of the responsibility incumbent upon them to lead with care and integrity.

SKILLS OF THE LEADER

Spiritual leaders—those in professional roles and lay leaders—are well served if they have an appreciation for the variety of ways people express their spiritual life. In mainline Protestant churches—where many members are just now discovering the theological significance of practices that foster spiritual growth—leaders can help people understand the spiritual gifts and resources they can already claim.

Those who teach spiritual practices will ordinarily want to have first experienced the practice being taught. This gives the leader an opportunity to know experientially what it is like to be in the learner's role. I offer a word of caution: Those who have experienced a particular practice favorably often assume, especially if they are new to spiritual practices, that all persons will react as favorably. It is important to recognize that leaders bring to an experiential practice their own life experiences and ways of reacting, but others may not experience the practice in the same way. As noted in the previous chapter, our spiritual practices open us to the Spirit, but they do not determine the way in which the Spirit will move.

People who are asked to teach spiritual exercises need to remember that having experienced an exercise does not necessarily qualify one to teach it even if one has found the exercise meaningful. In the same sense that going to school does not necessarily qualify one to be a teacher, so too experiencing spiritual practices does not necessarily mean that one can effectively lead others. A leader's skills are an important factor in determining what can be appropriately taught. Those who have much experience of the spiritual life, who have worked to build and nurture their own experiential relationship with God, who have been in discussions with others about their journey, and who have some experience as a religious leader will likely be more effective teachers of spiritual practices. The teacher's commitment to her or his own spiritual life is a central factor. Being attentive to one's own spiritual life and faithfully engaging in one's own spiritual disciplines keep one open to the leading of the Spirit. It takes dedication, energy, commitment, and a willingness to be vulnerable to the mystery that surrounds us all. When we are open to the Spirit's movement in our own lives, there is a greater potential for being open to the movement of the Spirit in the lives of others.

People from the helping professions—for example, psychologists, counselors, and social workers who faithfully attend to their own spiritual lives—are often excellent teachers. Those who have had pastoral counseling training or who are sensitive to the gifts associated with being an active listener will likely draw on this training if they teach spiritual practices. Programs for training spiritual directors are emerging at the present time. Summer school programs at a variety of theological schools frequently offer courses in spiritual direction and spiritual discernment. This training is crucial to those who want to devote considerable parts of their professional lives to spiritual guidance.

Occasionally, church leaders assume that because they are familiar with teaching techniques or active listening skills they can—without training or study—readily become good spiritual guides. Poor advice or guidance, however, can be harmful both spiritually and emotionally to those seeking guidance. A body of literature exists that draws on the insights, experiences, and practices of those who have dedicated their lives to spiritual growth and development. The professional spiritual leader ignores this literature not only to her or his personal peril, but also to the peril of those being led.

However, although training programs are valuable, not all teachers of spiritual practices need be graduates of such programs. Those who work on their spiritual lives in small peer group settings will learn from the intimacy of their sharing. Such groups where people are often friends or close associates provide a level of support and discernment that is often impossible in larger church settings. Clergy who have some training in spiritual direction can also teach other congregational leaders the skills needed to teach spiritual practices. The spiritual exercises contained in the next chapter can readily be used by church groups.

CONTEXT

Context played a major role in the camp communion service described at the beginning of this chapter. A storm could have raged outside a small chapel or a large mess hall while communion was being celebrated, and it is unlikely it would have had the same emotional impact it had on the outdoor service. The spiritual practice—communion—was being conducted in a format that enhanced its spiritual impact. Yet in this case, because the leaders were not sufficiently sensitive to the changing weather conditions, the context rather than the communion became the focus.

Leaders who are planning to teach spiritual practices need to recognize the impact the context may exert on participants. If attendees have positive feelings about the church or retreat center from past educational experiences offered there, they will probably come with positive expectations. Although most participants in educational programs begin with some initial anxiety, having positive expectations will help alleviate some of their fears. The converse is also true: If you are holding an event in surroundings unfamiliar to a group, the process of finding and settling into the new location will generate anxiety for some persons. Because spiritual practices generally require a heightened level of comfort for maximum effectiveness, allowing people ample opportunity to "settle in" and in some cases voice their anxiety is essential.

The room or specific area in which an exercise is taught will significantly influence the training process. Although not all people are sensitive to their surroundings, many will be assisted in the learning experience if the room sets a receptive tone. Does the room have a welcoming feel? A quiet atmosphere? What does the room "say," or how does it make you "feel" when you enter? Are the colors in the room inviting? Is the room orderly, or is part of the room used for storage? If you are attentive to these factors, you will know how much the room itself supports your goals and what you may need to do to alter the atmosphere. Occasionally leaders arrive at the last minute for the programs they are responsible for leading. If they know little about the space, they may be surprised to learn that its color, shape, or size does not contribute to their teaching goals.

If your aim is to help people focus, you may need to bring a candle or material to create a worship table for a focal point. Rooms that offer little support to the teaching of spiritual practices can often be claimed by the participants by having the group itself contribute to the environment. Members can be asked to bring from home things that are special to them or that they use to assist their own devotional life. Taking time for people to share something about the objects they bring can be an important source of spiritual nurture. If the event is being held in a retreat or camp setting, often the group can find objects in the natural world—for example, unusually shaped rocks, colorful leaves—that contribute to the room where the sessions will be held.

Leaders need to be aware of a room's environment, because it influences participation in spiritual practices, especially if

there is a problem. Praying, sharing, and group discussions require people to be alert and focused. Participants with the best
of intentions may find themselves fighting to stay awake or
distracted by their discomfort if the room is too hot or stuffy.
Air flow through a window or ventilation system can be a welcome treat in a warm room. A cold room can be just as difficult. Relaxation exercises taught on a cold floor, for instance,
are usually ineffective. Some leaders get so caught up in their
teaching that they fail to monitor the changing environment of
a room. This can be especially problematic if the room was fine
as things began, but over the course of a morning or afternoon
has changed. The leader needs to consciously notice what participants require to maximize their learning.

The context also shapes what is possible in terms of learning designs. What size room is appropriate to the learning
needs? If you have a large group, will the spiritual practice you
plan to teach require dividing into smaller groups? If so, will
you have the use of other small rooms, or is your assigned room
large enough to accommodate small groups with sufficient
space between them? Teaching spiritual practices requires having the space necessary for their use. A helpful spiritual practice is easily rendered useless if the space required for doing it
is inappropriate.

In some instances, being aware of the environment surrounding your learning space is a prerequisite. Practices that
require collecting objects from the natural world may be ideal
for camp settings but more difficult to obtain if one is teaching in the small basement room of an urban church. Also, when
considering your context, do not forget the noise factor. If you
are teaching spiritual practices that require quiet reflection and
you discover that in the room next to yours "Active Games for
Young Children" is being taught, it may be impossible to obtain an environment that supports your project. For groups that
require silence and reflection, the presence of noise in a nearby
location need not destroy the program, but it requires careful
treatment.

Some years ago I was participating in a group that met weekly
at 7 A.M. for an hour. Our leader was teaching us a variety of
spiritual practices. As it happened, we met in the small chapel

of a large mainline church. Outside the door, a homeless man slept each night in an alcove protected from the elements. Our arrival usually awakened him, and although he greeted us warmly, it would take him some time to pull his things together and begin the day. As our practices began, we could hear him start to mumble outside the door; as his emotional agitation increased, he would talk loudly to himself and frequently yell or curse. Our leader encouraged us to listen in the silence for this man's needs, pray for him, and be reminded that his voice was a call to each of us to work for a just society where people would not be forced to live on the streets. In that group we learned many spiritual practices, but we also learned how the nonsensical ranting of a homeless man could be the voice of the crucified God. Context counts: it can be an avenue for God's self-revelation as well as a distraction that keeps us from hearing God's voice.

THE USE OF TECHNOLOGICAL RESOURCES

Music, art, slides, videotapes, and materials from the Internet can be useful aids in teaching spiritual practices. Sometimes these wonderful avenues for opening the human spirit to the presence of the holy are overlooked or ignored. As noted in Chapter 1, human beings are created both matter and spirit. Often music and art are avenues to the soul; they evoke in us a sense of profound gratitude and joy. They make us aware that God is present in the depths of our bodies and spirits as well as in our world.

In my own teaching of spiritual practices, I have used the spiritual "Great Day" sung by Kathleen Battle and Jessye Norman[1] with nature slides taken by a friend who is a nature photographer. On numerous occasions, after using "Great Day"—with slides focused on the great day that existed as each of the animals was created—I have had people come up to me and say, "I don't know what happened when you showed these slides with the music, but I suddenly found tears welling up in my eyes." Something in the glory and beauty of the voices and images had deeply touched their spirits. For those so moved, this was another invitation to deepen their relationship with

God. Even for those not moved in this way, the experience filled a pleasant few minutes, but one must acknowledge that for some it may have been boring. What matters is that leaders do what they can to help people discover anew God's invitation. Remember that not everyone is helped by any given approach. If as a leader you think each practice has to "work" (that is, be helpful to everyone), you may want to examine your own unrealistic hopes as well as the freedom of the Spirit.

On another occasion a leader was using slides set to the music of "Simple Gifts." Everything had been tried before hand, and all was ready. A lunch break was to be followed with "Simple Gifts" as a way to draw the focus back to the spiritual practices of the afternoon. When the leader touched all the pre-arranged buttons, the slides appeared and the spiritual "Deep River" filled the room. After the initial shock, the projector and compact disc player were stopped. After a few minutes of fumbling, everyone in the room realized it was going to be impossible to get these coordinated in a timely fashion. Spontaneously, a woman with a strong soprano voice began singing "Simple Gifts." As the group joined in, the slides were quickly started, and a moment that had all the markings of disaster became a moment of grace. The simple gift of the voice had made the impressive technological equipment secondary.

Technological mishaps may be invitations to the Holy Spirit, as this one was. In general, however, if you are using technological equipment such as VCRs, slide projectors, and compact discs in your teaching and programming, be sure you understand how each piece of equipment works. Set it up ahead of time in the room you will be using, and make certain it works there, too. Nothing is more wonderful than the high notes of a Battle and Norman duet. Nothing is less helpful than a compact disc player that is so soft that these notes cannot be heard, or so loud that they blow people out of the room. Any program that requires the coordination of two pieces of equipment needs to be tested before participants arrive. Starting on the wrong slide or selection of music insures that the next several moments will be spent fumbling and bumbling around. This changes the attitude of expectancy in the participants to one of amusement or, if it goes on long enough, to frustration and disappointment.

PERSONAL CHARACTERISTICS OF THE PARTICIPANTS

If the camp episode that opened this chapter had involved adults rather than teens, the outcome would no doubt have been considerably altered. Adults would likely have responded to the storm with less anxiety and a willingness to finish their communion service in a camp building. Adults would also have been able to assimilate and integrate the general emotional climate more readily than did the teenagers. Saying good-bye to friends at the closing of the event would probably not carry the emotional valence that it did for the young people. Such factors as age, maturity, life experience, and judgment are all personal factors that influence the way in which spiritual practices are taught and experienced. It will be helpful to list some of these factors and briefly describe their significance.

Age

It is essential that spiritual practice teachers take into account the ages of people in the group. Is this a group for teens? For older adults? A mixed group? Age is a factor both in the selection of appropriate spiritual practices and in the methods used for teaching. Practices that are geared for one age may not be helpful with others. For example, in Chapter 2 we described a spiritual practice that used the imagination to "let go" of cherished personal attributes and beliefs. Teens and young adults who are in the process of building their egos may not benefit from a practice geared to those who are beginning the process of "letting go" of ego needs. Adults who have reached middle age or beyond are more suitably led in this practice.

On the other hand, many spiritual practices are containers waiting to be filled by the personal experience and history of the participants. In such cases the exercise is appropriate for a wide audience. These spiritual practices allow each person to move at her or his own pace. Most of the spiritual practices in this book are general enough that they can be adapted for use with a variety of ages. Some practices can be useful for a variety of ages with minimal adaptation. For example, relaxation exercises can usually be easily taught to young people and adults. If one were teaching relaxation exercises to a church seniors group, the exercises would need to be modified to accommodate their physical capabilities.

If discussion groups are used as part of the training process, the questions must be structured to elicit the interests and knowledge of the group. For example, a group of adults who are well versed in the history and polity of their religious tradition may be quite happy to reflect on Martin Luther or John Wesley's spirituality. Unchurched or younger groups not familiar with this history would lack the background needed to discuss such questions. On the other hand, young people who had been to a Rave service might be able to talk about the spiritual significance of this experience, whereas their elders would ask, "What is Rave?" As analysts of North American culture name and describe our various generations, such as Baby Boomers and Generation X, we increasingly recognize that people sitting next to each other in a discussion group may bring very different cultural expectations and assumptions. Generational differences need to be considered when teaching spiritual practices and when shaping discussion questions.

Readiness for Involvement

The motivation of the participants is a crucial factor in the use of spiritual practices. Some people are highly motivated; they come to a program focused on spirituality because of their personal interests or needs. They are eager to participate and if they have had some experience with spiritual practices are often willing to share that experience as appropriate.

In a large mainline Canadian congregation some years ago, the interest in spirituality was increasing; many parishioners had discovered quiet retreats held at a nearby Roman Catholic house of prayer. Eventually, the adult education committee of this congregation decided to sponsor a six-week series of programs on spiritual practices. One of the leaders suggested teaching relation exercises as a helpful first step. After discovering that this could involve lying on the floor, some church leaders were hesitant. Would some of the older members accept this? More specifically, a particular woman was identified as interested in the series but likely to be reticent about lying on the floor. Someone in the planning group said, "Look, Ms. X is interested in this stuff. Can you make lying on the floor optional and see how people respond?" The leader assured the committee that this would be possible, and plans progressed. The evening of the first event, when it came time to teach relaxation practices, the leader first got on the floor and casually demonstrated how it worked. When the invitation was extended to the group, the older person in question was one of the first to push her chair back and make herself comfortable on the floor. That particular night to a person the group learned physical relaxation lying on the floor.

The goal was to teach the practice in a way that insured that people were comfortable. If some people had felt more comfortable in their chairs or in some other position, that too would have been fine. Giving people options and maintaining a level of comfort are always important for a prayerful mood with spiritual practices. Highly motivated groups are often eager to participate; their fears about learning something new may be minimized by their interest in the topic.

Not all church groups are as highly motivated as the one described above. Some persons come to church-related events because they feel an obligation to support the minister, other church leaders, or a particular program of the church. Programs in the area of spirituality in smaller congregations may draw persons who are there because they feel obligated to support the church. Others are "testing the waters." They want to know if there is something here for them, but they come with a certain reluctance or anxiety. They come with concerns: Will I be asked questions about my spiritual life that might embarrass me? Will I be the only one who is not sure what spirituality means? Will I be asked to pray in a way I don't understand or can't relate to?

Spiritual leaders need to have a sense of humility and an understanding that God loves all of us for who we are, just as we are. Here we see the influence of the theological notion of "justification by faith" that was explored in Chapter 1. Although as spiritual leaders we are asking people to stretch and grow and deepen their relationship with the divine (the work of sanctification), we honor who people are and recognize that God is at work in their lives in ways we will never know. By honoring people's spirituality, we allow God to do the work; we see ourselves as people on the journey, even called at times to lead, but we see God's work as God's work.

Mainline Protestants frequently need to be led gently on this path. The years of defining themselves against evangelicals created a climate in which developing a personal relationship with God was anathema. Knowing how to help people walk gently into new spiritual territory is a gift that mainline Protestant leaders need to acquire and celebrate.

Physical Abilities and Limitations

As we become more aware of the variety of ways people are differently abled, we must consider this when teaching spiritual practices. This includes not asking people to do anything that they might be unable to do or that might be injurious to them.

A wise leader always reminds people in a group—regardless of their ages—that they should not do anything that they fear will impair their health. For example, persons with back problems should not be asked to do exercises or body movements that might aggravate their condition. If a group decided that fasting was a spiritual practice they would like to try during Lent, the leader would want to remind people with diabetes, hypoglycemia, or other physical conditions to avoid doing anything that would precipitate illness. Fasting as a spiritual discipline can be practiced in a number of ways: for a few hours to a number of days; eating and drinking only fluids; eating smaller portions; skipping one meal a day. The many ways fasting can be practiced demonstrate the flexibility and adaptability of most spiritual disciplines.

Gender

When teaching spiritual practices, the gender of the participants is also an important issue. Men's or women's groups in the church may make use of spiritual practices that address their specific concerns or needs. Practices designed for women or men may be especially useful. Although not the focus of this work, resources for these groups can be acquired from bookstores that serve mainline Protestants' publishing needs.

Many church settings in which spiritual practices are used will involve mixed groups. Those who lead spiritual practices will be well served to have some knowledge of developmental psychology, especially as it relates to the differences in personal development fostered by cultural norms and practices. Men in general are not socialized toward emotional sensitivity. Much of developmental psychology prior to the last twenty years chronicled men's development and assumed it was also normative for women. As the women's movement has progressed and shaped studies of women, it is clear that the developmental path for women is not the same as that for men. Men, for example, first learn to be assertive and claim their goals and aspirations as they relate to the external world and then later develop the capacity for intimacy. For women this is reversed. Skills for intimacy and bonding generally occur first, followed by a mastery of the external world.

Men and women have different styles of communication, different ways of expressing emotions, different ways of expressing intimacy. Knowing something of these differences will help leaders effectively lead spiritual practices.

For example, it is common for those who feel God's presence in the depths of their joys or sorrows to express this with tears. For men who have been socialized not to cry—at least not in public—this gift of tears may be frightening. Women who have been socialized to serve others rather than express and seek their own fulfillment may initially be uncomfortable if their spiritual insights lead toward assertive behavior in the service of personal goals and personal fulfillment.

If the group is mixed and personal sharing is an aspect of the spiritual practice, the leader will need to be sensitive to the needs of both women and men. There may be a tendency in mixed groups for certain experiences to be valued more than others, for example, men's experiences over women's experiences. The spiritual leader needs to help groups understand that God is at work in the lives of all people; no particular set of circumstances or life experiences is more valuable than are others.

THE SPIRITUAL PRACTICES

Those who teach and lead spiritual practices need to know the background and theological significance of the practices being used. Can the spiritual practice be used with integrity? Does it reflect the Protestant tradition? Because spiritual practices do reflect certain theological traditions and perspectives, it is important for the leaders to have some knowledge of the theological assumptions they may implicitly be teaching through their use of given practices. This is not to say, however, that Protestants cannot use Roman Catholic spiritual practices. Protestants need to claim the first sixteen centuries of the church as their own. Many practices in the pre-Reformation period of church history can be reclaimed without violating Protestant principles or beliefs. Spiritual practices from other faiths may also be useful. Such practices, however, need to be understood in the context of the traditions from which they come.

Spiritual practices have an integrity that needs to be maintained. Although many practices can be amended or adjusted to meet the needs of a particular group or setting, they should not be subjected to the type of "cut and paste" approach that uses them as a hodgepodge of techniques. Spiritual practices are disciplines that have been used in many cases for a number of years to guide people on their spiritual journey. They are not intended as "nice little exercises" that can be used willy-nilly to "liven up a group"! The "we tried that last week, what will we do this week?" approach to spiritual practices undermines the integrity of the spiritual disciplines themselves and trivializes the lives of those who are using them.

Spiritual practices also vary greatly in their complexity. Some are easy to teach and require little effort to learn. Others involve several complex steps and must be practiced a number of times to gain comfort with them. Leaders need to have experienced the practices they are planning to teach, for it is as a participant that one recognizes what is required for proper instruction. Participants can often intuit if a leader knows the practice well. Spiritual leaders do not have to use every practice they teach as a part of their own daily disciplines. However, it is advisable to have gained—by personally using the practice—a sense of the teaching/learning issues involved. This familiarity makes it easier not only to teach the practice but also to answer questions that emerge in the teaching process.

THE TEACHING PROCESS

Spiritual exercises require time to teach and learn. Those who teach spiritual practices need to allow ample time for (1) teaching the practice, (2) setting the necessary mood for engaging in the practice, (3) experiencing the practice, and (4) debriefing. Failing to allow ample time for any of these steps can diminish the quality of the experience.

When teaching a spiritual practice, it is often helpful to have a handout prepared with the steps listed. This is especially important if the individuals or groups are expected to follow the steps without your guidance during the session. For example, Luther's Four-Stranded Garland provided in Chapter 4 requires a number of steps. Teaching this necessitates going over the steps as an initial introduction. Once people are using the steps in prayer, they often find being able to refer to a handout helps them follow the process.

Another format for teaching complicated practices to large groups involves dividing the large group into several small groups. All of the small groups remain in the same room, and the teaching is conducted from the front of the room. Although each small group would normally work as a self-contained unit and assume responsibility for the practice, in this model the leaders working from the front of the room simultaneously lead all the groups through the practice. A case in point is the Four-Stranded Garland, which requires five readings of a Scripture passage. When a small group uses this exercise, the members of the group take turns reading the passages so that each reading is in a different voice. When teaching this to a large group, however, it is helpful to break the participants into small groups while using five readers at the front of the room who can be heard by all the small groups. Readers need to speak loudly or be amplified so that they can be easily heard throughout the room. By quietly and prayerfully providing instructions from the front of the room throughout the exercise, the participant's anxiety regarding remembering each step is alleviated. If you have passed out instructions, some persons will rustle papers trying to follow along if they are not told that verbal guidance will be provided along the way. This teaching format keeps all the groups moving at approximately the same pace. If the spiritual practice is only one part of the program, having the groups somewhat synchronized facilitates movement into the next aspect of the program. Exercises that are likely to be led from the front of a room, such as guided meditations, will not require handouts during the initial learning process. These practices are straightforward enough that in most cases participants will have little difficulty following along. In these cases the use of the handout may come at the end of the exercise to facilitate the use of the practice during the week. The prayer of examen in the next chapter is an example of this type of spiritual practice. If you want to keep the group focused on your presentation, do not use a handout unless it is aimed at the outline of your presentation. Otherwise some people will read the handout rather than listen to your instructions.

After teaching the basics of a spiritual exercise, remember that the mood set by instruction is probably not the mood that will be required for effective use of the spiritual practice. Once participants' questions have been answered and puzzled looks eliminated, it is time to set the tone for the spiritual practice. If the spiritual practice requires quiet, ask the group to take a few moments to center or quiet themselves. If the practice requires movement within the room, leaving the room, or some other activity, it will be important to set the required tone before sending people out on their own. In some practices, discussion is required; for example, with the covenant-group practice in the next chapter. This discussion may require participants to do some "getting to know you" exercises before they can work well together. As a leader you will need to attend to the tone and help the group establish what is needed for the spiritual practice.

Next, allow ample time for the spiritual practice itself. Trying to rush either the teaching or doing of a spiritual practice usually renders it ineffective. If there are time constraints on the group, make certain that you have done the necessary planning to meet those constraints. The practices are designed to quiet the compulsive noise that clutters our lives, to open us to our deepest longings, and to establish a relationship with God; thus nothing could be more antithetical to the process than trying to rush the experience. If you are running out of time, amend your program; do a shorter exercise or carry over the postexercise phase.

Debriefing following a spiritual practice is also extremely important. It gives people an opportunity to consolidate their experiences by both reflecting on and verbalizing them. People, however, should not feel compelled to share with others in the group. Note too that what is being asked for is not the sharing of the contents of the spiritual experience—that is often too personal for sharing in this setting—but a reaction to the exercise itself. Was it helpful? In what way? If it was not helpful, share this. No exercise is always helpful to everyone. This sharing honors each person's experience and frees people from believing they must have a positive reaction to each practice.

Do not forget that in larger groups more time will be needed for questions, for discussion, if it is involved, and for debriefing. If the exercise selected is rather complicated, allow plenty of instruction time. With very large groups it may be necessary to use less complicated practices, unless the group is quite experienced.

RESOURCES FOR REFERRAL

Mental health professionals have long recognized the importance of the clergy as a source of referral for people seeking mental health counseling. For many years people have reported that when they are in trouble the pastor is the first professional person with whom difficulties are shared. It is also true that a number of people who participate in church programs have specific unmet needs that they may or may not recognize. Leaders of spiritual practices need to recognize the probability that some of the participants will surface issues requiring further pastoral or psychological counseling, or psychiatric attention.

As described in Chapter 2, spiritual growth and emotional growth are intimately related. When spiritual growth involves practices that move the participant into realms that have heretofore remained unconscious, substantive emotional and spiritual material may emerge that requires longer-term processing than the spiritual practice permits. For example, great care is required when using a guided imagery exercise to help people imagine the spirituality they inherited from their families of origin. Participants are asked to imagine how God was at work in their parents' home before their birth. What was their parents' relationship like? How did they express their joys and sorrows? What were God's hopes for them? How did their parents feel when they learned they were going to have a child? When they were born, did their parents feel great joy? When they were small children, how was God's love communicated to them by their parents?

Going through this guided imagery journey is a wonderful experience for many people. They gain a new appreciation of their parents, their family home, and the joy that they brought to their parents when they were born. For others this may be a very negative experience. For those who have not been fully aware of the negative aspects of their parental home, this may be an overwhelming experience. Through participation in the exercise, those who have been physically or sexually abused as children may access memories and fears more profoundly than previously experienced. Dealing with these emotional and spiritual agendas will probably be required for their healing, but attempting to deal with such issues in a gathering where the group contract does not include this depth of support (including a trained mental health leader) is inappropriate.

Professionally trained leaders know that before guiding people in exercises of this type it is important to give people permission to opt out at any time. They should be instructed or invited to stop participating in the guided journey if they begin to feel emotionally or spiritually overwhelmed. Participants can be invited to opt out by using their imaginations to go to another place or by physically leaving the room.

The spiritual practices of the next chapter are not intended to lead people specifically into emotionally charged areas. However, any spiritual practice has the potential to open people to areas of their lives that need healing. Sometimes people will be surprised by what emerges in prayer, in quiet, in devotional Bible study. Understanding the model of intrapsychic spiritual development described in Chapter 2 will make a leader aware of these issues. Alerting participants to the relationship between spiritual and emotional growth often removes some of the fear if emotionally difficult material emerges. It also is reassuring if the leader makes it clear that resources for referral are available should someone feel this would be helpful. Trained religious leaders will want to know which mental health professionals in the community value and take seriously spiritual issues.

GROUP PROCESS

Those who are trained in group process or who know something of how groups work will find that this information serves them well in the teaching of group activities. A crucial initial step involves establishing clearly understood goals and expectations that are mutually agreed upon by the leader and the participants. During the first session these expectations can be listed on a flip chart or a blackboard and can serve as a group contract. Is attendance expected at all sessions? How does the group feel about arriving on time? What are members expected to bring, for example, notebooks for keeping a journal or a Bible? Are people willing to participate in practices that are new? Are they willing to do some physical and spiritual stretching? Will the leader see to it that the sessions end on time so that people can leave promptly? In settings where people travel some distance to participate, this may be especially important.

What needs to happen for attendees to feel safe in the group? Ask the group what this means for them. Listing the suggestions on a flip chart helps preserve the needs and allows people to look them over to see if everyone concurs. Some suggestions may require negotiation. Permission to opt out of any exercise or discussion that does not feel comfortable helps people recognize they are not surrendering their personal power. Permission to leave the room, if necessary, is often reassuring. Once all the needs are listed, they can become part of the group's covenant.

With groups who do not know one another, it is important to spend time in group building. Giving people an opportunity to know one another increases the comfort level in the group. In mainline Protestant contexts, however, it is important to communicate very early in the group process that the focus of spiritual practices is the work of the Spirit. Providing time for group building may well come after an opening worship that directs the group to the presence of the Holy Spirit.

Mainline Protestant congregations are usually experienced with the games and techniques used as "ice breakers" for group building. Often the use of too many of these practices reinforces a focus on the group when the aim of the program is to assist people in developing their openness to the Spirit. Occasionally, this focus on the group itself can be found in both the worship and small-group life of mainline churches. It is typified by unspoken attitudes that suggest "we are such nice people, God's love is surely in our midst." The affirmation is no doubt true, but one senses that asking more specifically how or where God's love is present in their midst would elicit either puzzlement or a sentimental statement about how much "we like each other." In Chapter 1 we described how mainline Protestants have not been taught to discern God's presence in the midst of their daily lies. Their foundational attitudes toward the work of God have reinforced the idea that God is present with us when "two or three are gathered together," but only in a nebulous, undergirding manner. Helping groups recognize that the Spirit is in the midst of their group life and in the midst of their daily lives may be a new focus for a number of mainline Protestants.

Groups can readily be taught to discern God's presence calling them to faithfulness—to faithful attitudes, beliefs, and actions—in their corporate and individual contexts. Once a group begins to recognize this, a period of check-in each week can be a source of personal support and a rich source of spiritual enrichment. When groups form to participate on a regular basis in spiritual practices, they frequently develop a deep bond. This bond is built not primarily by group-building practices but on the trust that develops when persons share the profound movement of God's work in their lives. Now the time of sharing becomes more than seeking support by telling others our stories; it becomes an opportunity to hear our stories and the stories of others with an eye to the work of the Spirit in our daily lives. The depth this may touch is often quite profound. Warmth, mutual support, and personal transformation are present, but they are not the focus. Attention to the working of the Holy Spirit in our midst keeps us growing in faithfulness.

SPIRITUAL GROWTH FOR THE CONGREGATION

As noted in Chapter 1, there is a tendency on the part of mainline Protestants to be skeptical in their attitudes toward spirituality. Some people will be threatened by the term. Others will dismiss spiritual concerns without much knowledge or awareness of their purpose or value. Although this cannot be prevented, those who are responsible for spiritual leadership need to be able to respond to this and avoid stances that will increase the fear or threat. A few suggestions that address this issue may be helpful.

Those responsible for the spiritual leadership of the congregation—professional and lay leaders—need to make certain that groups formed to promote spiritual growth are not seen as elitist. Established groups committed to spiritual practices often develop a deep level of bonding and trust. Over time they may fear jeopardizing this supportive climate and resist inviting others into the group. It is appropriate to offer programs for those who are experienced. However, as a general guideline I believe that new people should be welcomed if they attend knowing that the event is for persons experienced in spiritual practices. Publicity and descriptions of the program should reflect the nature of the series. If possible, the church's annual cycle of programs should include opportunities for beginners and newcomers who are seeking spiritual development. In this way those who are new to the practices will have an opportunity to learn, and those who have been working together on their spiritual development can continue to grow. The publicity about the spirituality offerings in congregational newsletters, fliers, and announcements needs to be explicit regarding the nature of the groups being offered.

A large mainline Protestant church with which I had some familiarity some years ago had an established group committed to spiritual development. Over the course of eight years they had grown together and valued their opportunities to build on what they had learned. Each year they spent at least one Saturday together at a retreat house in the community.

These leaders—most of whom were active on other church committees—always advertised these gatherings as opportunities for spiritual growth. Occasionally new people did attend. Some found the retreats helpful, and others felt it was "over their head." People with both types of experiences came away feeling they were valued by the group. In any case, opportunities for spiritual growth were planned as part of the adult education program.

I remember hearing about a person who came to a weekend retreat and by midmorning recognized she did not have enough experience with extended periods of silence to feel comfortable. Before lunch she told the group at sharing time, "I'm not getting anything out of this right now. I'm going to stay for lunch, and if I don't get anything from the next period I'm going to go and come again another year after I've had more experience with silence." Then she smiled and said, "Or I might not come again!" Laughter filled the room, and to a person the group told her in a variety of ways that she was welcome to stay as long as she wanted and in the future to come back if she wanted to try it again. I did not hear if she returned another year. It did not matter. Either way, she was personally affirmed and her role in the congregation validated.

Groups committed to spiritual growth periodically need to do a spiritual checkup on themselves. One thing they will want to avoid is fostering holier-than-thou attitudes in their members. Because many mainline Protestants do not feel called to attend spiritual-growth groups, there is occasionally a tendency on the part of those so called to feel a bit privileged. Those who are involved need to remember that they are not more valued in God's eyes than those who are not involved. As mainline Protestants, we affirm a belief in justification by faith, not works. Our spiritual practices help us grow in response to the many gifts we have received from God, but they do not make us more worthy than those who are involved in other ministries of the church. Those who are participating may need to be reminded of this. It is common for people who have a new spiritual insight or feel a new depth to their relationship with God to be so excited that they share indiscriminately. Others who have not had such experiences may hear this as boasting, or they may feel inadequate. Humility is an important gift of the

Spirit that must not to be overlooked even in the midst of personal excitement and transformation. Helping people who participate in groups committed to spiritual development recognize that their contribution to the overall life of the church is no more or less than that of other groups will avoid a spiritual elitism that is neither becoming nor faithful. Spiritual practices are intended to help us conform to the will of God by being true to our deepest self, the self we are in God.

The guidelines and suggestions offered in this chapter are intended to provide helpful background information for those who teach and lead spiritual practices. Leaders with little experience may find these especially helpful. Although this chapter is not intended as a comprehensive cataloguing of all the necessary preparations for serving as a spiritual guide, it provides the necessary background for leading the exercises that follow.

4

Spiritual Practices

INTRODUCTION

This chapter includes a number of spiritual practices that either emerge from the Protestant tradition or are consonant with it. Each practice is preceded by a section that provides the theological or historical background that undergirds the practice. Directions are provided for leaders who will be using the practices as well as instructions to use for teaching spiritual practices. Because most of these descriptions are designed for teaching spiritual practices to small groups, some implications for individual use will be provided as appropriate.

RELAXATION EXERCISES

Background

Relaxation exercises have a number of uses including preparation for prayer. People who suffer from hypertension (high blood pressure) or who have had heart attacks often learn relaxation practices in order to improve their physical health. They are useful, as well, for reducing emotional stress and reducing insomnia. Learning what Dr. Herbert Benson calls the relaxation response is also helpful for deepening one's prayer life. Learning how to relax (and ironically enough, one does need to learn to relax) allows a person to change her or his threshold of attention. Relaxation slows down the body's autonomic system (for example, breathing, heart rate) and shifts one's attention.

For most people this happens spontaneously from time to time in the natural course of events. You may have gone outside on a night that was especially still. Perhaps starlight filled the sky. Suddenly you noticed you could hear things from far away that you normally would not notice. There may have been a certain quality about the evening. Perhaps the air was calm or there was a gentle breeze, and although you were in a familiar place the atmosphere and sounds seemed different. Your threshold of attention may also have been transformed.

People who enjoy trips to natural settings, remote woods or parks, often report that they notice things—the songs of birds or the sounds of animals—that normally escape their attention. Here again the threshold of attention is changed; there is a stillness both inside and outside the body that allows them to perceive things that heretofore went unnoticed.

The quality of changing our threshold of attention is the gift that relaxation exercises bring to prayer. They teach us to slow down, listen, and attend to cues that in the busyness of our lives go unnoticed. If God is an active agent in our daily lives, our call as people of faith is to discern where God's creative, transforming work of love is being embodied. Occasionally God does appear to get our attention by dramatic means (the wind and fire method!), but more often than not the subtlety of the "still small voice" tries to break into our lives. If we are unable to stop, listen and hear because of the noise that surrounds us, we miss opportunities to walk in concert with God's gentle, guiding Spirit.

The pace and demands on us keep us numb to life's deeper significance. Our consumer-driven society tells us—via the television—what we need and how we should spend our time. An idle moment is anathema! Being overworked or too busy are the sins we love to claim! Have you noticed that if you ask people if they were busy last week most give an emphatic "yes"? If you then inquire about the nature of the activity, often they cannot remember what they were doing! Relaxation exercises are a partial antidote to the numbing distractions that encompass many of our lives. As an aid to prayer, these exercises facilitate listening to our deepest longings and needs. By focusing our attention on our bodies or our minds, they remind us that life is more than activity, no matter how altruistic or important we deem our activities.

Physical and Mental Relaxation Exercises

There are many types of relaxation exercises.[1] Not every type is helpful to everyone. Remember, it takes practice to find the benefit; if you try a relaxation exercise and it is not immediately helpful, do not be discouraged. These exercises must be practiced to be learned. On the other hand, if you have tried an exercise four or five times and you find it utterly unhelpful, you will probably want to try another type of practice. Some are designed to quiet the mind; others focus on the body. You can focus your attention on an image, on tensing and relaxing various muscle groups throughout your body, on imaging in your mind each part of your body moving to a state of peace and calm. Some relaxation practices are very similar to prayer practices. Guided imagery can be employed to relax in preparation for prayer (going to a quiet spot for a sense of warmth and support) or for prayer itself (imagine a conversation in which you speak with Jesus about a particular concern). Find one or two relaxation exercises that are helpful, and in the early stages of prayer consider making them a part of your spiritual discipline.

A script for a basic physical relaxation exercise and suggestions for using a mental relaxation practice follow. These have been used by many people for a number years. I include them not because they are unique or better than others, but because I have used them with a number of groups with positive response.

I want to add some words of caution about these practices. If you have medical conditions that preclude doing some of the physical activities described in the relaxation exercise, do not do them. Some people have backs that "go out" or limbs or muscles that should not be exercised in particular ways. If you have a condition that prevents you from doing any part of the exercise, skip that part of the practice and move to the other aspects in which you can participate. Also, for a few people (a small but stable percent), physical relaxation exercises increase rather than reduce anxiety. If you find a particular type of practice increases your level of stress, do not use it. Becoming more anxious defeats the purpose of the practice and will not assist you in your preparation for prayer.

Physical Relaxation Exercises

Instructions for the Leader

If you, as the leader, want participants to have the opportunity to do the relaxation exercise on the floor, move to the floor and demonstrate the exercises while discussing them. Make certain people can see and hear. Show the group how to tense and relax each of the muscle groups: wrinkling up the forehead, bending the arms, tilting the head back, pushing out on the abdomen, pulling in the buttocks, pushing the toes forward. If you do this in front of the group, anxiety is relieved and people know precisely what will be asked of them. Invite participants to skip any practice that would cause physical or emotional discomfort. People with bad backs or fibromyalgia may need to opt out of some of these; people who have been sexually abused may find that something in the exercise triggers disturbing memories.

The directions that follow are to be read slowly, allowing ample time for each aspect of the practice. Adopting a uniform voice tone and steady pace while moving through the tensing and relaxing aspects of the practice establishes a soothing rhythm that itself contributes to the experience of relaxation. It also invites people to give themselves over emotionally to the practice.

Instructions for the Participants

1. Find a comfortable place on the floor lying on your back. (People who prefer to remain in a chair for health reasons or personal comfort should be invited to do so.) Make certain there is ample room for you to move your arms and legs. If you are doing this with a group, make certain you will not be encroaching on the space of people next to you. Take a few moments to notice your body and how it feels. How does your clothing feel? Is anything too tight around your waist or your neck? Loosen tight-fitting clothing as appropriate until you feel comfortable.

2. Now take a few moments to check on your emotional space. Are you preoccupied with anything? A work project? A relationship? If you feel preoccupied with something, take a few moments and give this over to God for the duration of the exercise. Whatever it is, you can return to it at a later time.

3. Now take a few moments to simply enjoy the quiet. If you have experience with centering yourself, take time now to do that. If you do not have that experience, simply notice the change in the room from activity to quiet. You may notice

sounds outside the room or the breathing and rustling of others in the room. Notice these sounds and allow yourself to notice again the contrast between activity and quiet. If you feel comfortable closing your eyes and you have not already done so, feel free to close your eyes. If you feel uncomfortable with your eyes closed, stare at a fixed point on the ceiling (if lying down) or floor (if seated).

4. We will begin now the muscle relaxation exercise starting first with our fingers and hands. Clench your hands tightly into fists. Feel the tension in your fingers and hands as you make a fist. Hold the tension. Concentrate on the tension. And now relax and feel the contrast between tension and relaxation. Once again clench your hands into fists. Feel the tension in your fists. Hold the tension. Concentrate on the tension. And now relax and feel the contrast between tension and relaxation.

5. Now with your arms down along your sides, stretch your arms straight out. Feel the tension along your arms as you stretch them straight out. Hold the tension. Focus on the tension. And now relax. Enjoy the contrast between tension and relaxation. Now hold your arms straight out and feel the tension in your arms while letting your fingers and hands remain relaxed. Hold the tension. Focus on the tension. And now relax. Enjoy the contrast between tension and relaxation.

6. Now bend your arms at the elbows so that your biceps are tense. Focus on the tension in your biceps. Hold the tension. Focus on the tension. And now relax. Enjoy the contrast between tension and relaxation. Again bend your arms at the elbows, focusing the tension in your biceps. Focus on the tension in your biceps while the rest of your arm and hands remain relaxed. Concentrate on the tension. Hold the tension. And now relax and enjoy the contrast between tension and relaxation.

7. While lying quietly, feel the relaxation in your fingers. Let the relaxation in your fingers spread across the palms of your hands; let the relaxation move around your wrists and into your lower arms. Let the relaxation spread up your lower arms

and around your elbows. Let it move up into your upper arms, across the biceps, and into your shoulders. Enjoy the feeling of relaxation in your hands and arms.

8. While letting your hands and arms feel relaxed, focus the tension in your forehead by scrunching up your forehead. You may do this by trying to look at the top of your head. Feel the tension in your forehead. Hold the tension. Focus on the tension. And now relax and enjoy the contrast between tension and relaxation. Again scrunch up your forehead. Feel the tension across your forehead. Focus on the tension. And now relax and feel the contrast between tension and relaxation.

9. Now feel the tension around your eyes by gently but firmly closing your eyes. Hold the tension around your eyes. Focus on the tension. And now relax and enjoy the contrast between tension and relaxation. Repeat.

10. Now focus the tension in your mouth by pressing your tongue against the roof of your mouth. Focus on the tension in your tongue and mouth. Feel the tension. Concentrate on the tension. And now relax. Enjoy the contrast between tension and relaxation. Repeat.

11. Now focus the tension in your jaw by clenching your teeth together. Feel the tension in your jaw as you clench your teeth together. Hold the tension. Focus on the tension. And now relax. Enjoy the contrast between tension and relaxation. Repeat.

12. Now while your head remains relaxed, pull your chin down to your chest and feel the tension in the back of your neck. Focus on the tension. Hold the tension. And now relax and feel the contrast between tension and relaxation.

13. Now tilt your head back by lifting your chin and feel the tension in the front of your neck. Focus on the tension. Hold the tension. And now relax and feel the contrast between tension and relaxation. Repeat once.

14. Now feel the tension in your shoulders by pulling your shoulders straight up. While your arms remain relaxed, feel

the tension in your shoulders. Focus on the tension. Hold the tension. And now relax and enjoy the contrast between tension and relaxation. Repeat.

15. (Remember: Do not ask people to hold their breath.) Now feel the tension in your chest by very slowly inhaling a deep breath. Remember not to hold your breath. Feel the tension as you very, very slowly inhale. Feel the contrast between tension and relaxation as you very, very slowly exhale. Repeat.

16. Now focus the tension in your abdomen by pulling in your abdomen. Pull your abdomen in and feel the tension. Hold the tension. Focus on the tension. And now relax and enjoy the contrast between tension and relaxation. Repeat.

17. Now feel the tension in your abdomen by pushing out on your abdomen. Feel the tension across your abdomen as you push your muscles out. Hold the tension. Focus on the tension. Now relax. Enjoy the contrast between tension and relaxation. Repeat.

18. Now tense your buttocks. Clench your buttocks together and feel the tension. Focus on the tension. Hold the tension. Now relax and enjoy the contrast between tension and relaxation. Repeat.

19. Now feel the relaxation though your entire upper body. Let the relaxation move from your fingers into your palms. Let it move around your wrists and up your arms. Let the relaxation spread around your elbows and into your upper arms. Let the relaxation spread around your shoulders and up the back of your neck. Let the relaxation spread across your scalp, across your forehead, around your eyes, around your jaw, down your chin and the front of your neck. Let the relaxation spread across your chest and around your abdomen. Now that your upper body is completely relaxed, enjoy the feeling of relaxation. (Pause)

20. Now you can feel twice as relaxed by very, very slowly taking a deep breath and very, very slowly letting it out. (Pause) Enjoy the feeling of relaxation. (Pause)

21. Now while your upper body remains relaxed, focus the tension in the back of your legs by bending your ankles and pointing your toes toward your body. Feel the tension along the back of your leg as you bend your ankle. Hold the tension. Focus on the tension. Now relax and enjoy the contrast between tension and relaxation. Repeat.

22. Now focus the tension along the top of your legs by pointing your toes away from your body. Pointing your toes away from your body, feel the tension along the top of your legs. Focus on the tension. Hold the tension. And now relax and enjoy the contrast between tension and relaxation. Repeat.

23. Keeping your legs relaxed, make a fist with your feet. Feel the tension in your feet as you make a fist with your feet. Focus on the tension. Hold the tension. Now relax and enjoy the contrast between tension and relaxation. Repeat.

24. Now let the relaxation spread around your lower body. Feel the relaxation in your feet and ankles. Let the relaxation move up your legs, around your knees, into your thighs. Let the relaxation move into your abdomen, around your hips, around your waist. Let the relaxation gently move around your chest, across your shoulders, up your neck, around your jaw, eyes, and forehead. Let the relaxation flow down into your shoulders and upper arms. Let the relaxation spread around your elbows, into the palms of your hands, and into your fingers. (Pause) Now you are in a state of complete relaxation. Enjoy this feeling of relaxation. (Pause)

25. When you are ready to come back to this room, count backwards from three to one, and when you are ready, open your eyes. You will feel refreshed and relaxed. (Allow plenty of time for people to come back to the room. Allow them to stretch, stir, move about as needed as they come back together as a group.)

Once people have returned to their former positions in the group (probably sitting in chairs), allow people to reflect on the experience. Did they feel relaxed? What helped? What did not? Would they want to use this again in their own preparation time for prayer?

Mental Relaxation Exercises

Mental relaxation exercises require using the imagination to relax selected muscle groups. Instead of tensing and relaxing each set of muscles, as in physical relaxation practices, the participants are given a few moments to imagine relaxing each area of the body, for example, fingers, hands, arms, and so forth. Using the muscle groups provided in the physical relaxation script, the leader slowly leads people through the practice using warm relaxing voice tones and a uniform rhythm to create a climate of relaxation.

Mental relaxation is especially useful with people who find that physical exercises increase anxiety; with people who have physical conditions that prevent them from tensing muscle groups; and in settings where it is difficult to provide ample floor space for participants. Mental relaxation exercises also can be practiced privately; for example, on public transit or in other settings where it would be impossible to reduce tension using physical relaxation exercises.

Individual and Group Use

The exercises provided can be done either alone or with a group. An experienced group leader can use the script provided above and successfully lead people through the practice. If doing this with a group, be certain there is space on the floor to accommodate the group. Also, make certain participants will be able to make the floor comfortable. Is the floor carpeted? Will they need pillows or small rugs? Is the room temperature suitable?

Individuals can use a script to learn the practice, or they can tape-record the script and play it back using their own voices as the guide. There are many commercial versions of relaxation exercises available on tape. Some are for physical relaxation; others are for mental relaxation. Discover what helps you.

RULE OF LIFE

Background

A Rule of Life is a list of practices and activities used to express one's faithfulness to God and to nurture one's spiritual life. Although the notion of a rule to guide spiritual growth and development sounds rigid and severe in the contemporary context, it is helpful to think of rules as guidelines for ordering daily life. Creating a personal Rule of Life promotes spiritual development by increasing our awareness of the many things we do to nourish our spirits. The Rule of Life can help us evaluate our spiritual practices, assess the nature of our personal commitments, and claim the often unrecognized spiritual significance of many of our daily activities.

The notion of a Rule of Life dates to the early centuries of the Christian church. The term was used by the earliest monastic communities to describe the way in which they organized their daily life as individuals and as a community. Wanting to take seriously Paul's admonition to "pray without ceasing" (1 Thess. 5:17), they created an order to their day that included corporate and personal prayer as well as work and study. By the fifth century a number of formal Rules developed to guide monastic living patterns that were emerging. The Rule of Benedict, established circa 540 by Benedict of Nursia, drew elements from earlier Rules. It gained widespread acceptance among monastic communities and remains influential to the present day.

Protestant reformers—with their desire to transform ecclesiastical institutions and practices—were more interested in closing monastic communities than in creating new Rules for Christian living.[2] Yet the notion of ordering our daily life around our faith commitments endures through the creation of books of order and worship. For example, *The Book of Common Prayer* of the Episcopal Church presents a model for daily life and orients the believer to a life of faithfulness. By creating books that order patterns of worship and prayer—for example, *The Book of Order* (Presbyterian) or Chalice Worship[3] (Disciples of Christ)—Protestants are offered resources for ordering and nurturing the spiritual life. From frequently celebrated services of daily and weekly prayer and Eucharist, each with its accompanying scriptural readings, to the less frequently celebrated services of marriage and burial, the routine and extraordinary events of daily life are anchored in the community of faith. Viewing mainline Protestant books of prayer and worship from the perspective of a Rule of Life opens the believer to the deeper significance these resources offer in shaping a life of faithfulness. In more recent times, creating a "rule" individually or in small groups serves as a means for highlighting the importance of relating our faith to our daily life.

Use of the Practice

Although Protestants at the end of the twentieth century do not intend to create rules for living in monastic communities, the rediscovery of the spiritual significance of a Rule of Life provides another avenue for spiritual growth. Making explicit the rule by which our lives are implicitly lived provides an opportunity to reflect upon and shape the ways we nurture our spirits. Making a Rule of Life simply involves listing the things we do to nurture our spirit. As a leader I have heard items from many lists, including: caring for my garden, quiet time alone in the car while commuting, listening to music (not necessarily religious), taking time to look in my child's eyes, serving meals to those with AIDS, caring for a pet, going to church on a regular basis, being part of a Bible study group, doing dishes, doing volunteer work, making love, taking time for friends, walking by the ocean, watching the sunset, spending time gazing at works of art, dancing, praying with a special object, making an altar for one's home, traveling to sacred places, remembering friends who offered spiritual and emotional support. Often these lists contain activities people had either taken for granted or not previously associated with the nourishment of their spirit. Awakening them to the spiritual significance of activities previously viewed as merely "enjoyable" or "fun" adds a new dimension to daily life. The activities themselves become avenues for spiritual nurture and growth, and the relationship with the sacred is deepened through the process.

Other surprises sometimes emerge. I remember working with a group of religious professionals when someone in the group noticed that not a single person had put anything on the list that had to do with organized religious activities. This led them to ask why and to explore ways events for which they provided leadership might be enriched or made more meaningful.

Creating a personal Rule of Life also allows one to look seriously at the practices and events that open one to life's deeper levels of meaning. People seeking growth need to know what they already do well. Some may be shocked at how little they do to nourish their spirits. Others may be impressed to discover they do many things they had not previously acknowledged. Some people may want to add to their list, or do something more frequently, or stop doing something that does not help, or celebrate what they do now. The opportunity, not only to consciously reflect on one's implicit rules for living but also to celebrate these with others, serves to deepen one's spiritual life.

For those persons who want to use their Rule of Life as a basis for further spiritual development, a key ingredient of spiritual guidance requires taking small steps. A major difficulty people encounter when attempting spiritual growth is becoming discouraged when they attempt a major change they cannot achieve. Attempting large steps will almost always result in failure. For example, if you spend five minutes a day in silence and want to increase your quiet time, add another three to five minutes. Do not try to add fifteen or twenty minutes or you will likely not be successful. It would be too much too soon. I remember working with a woman who was an accomplished pianist with two small children. When she did her Rule of Life, she was surprised to notice that her piano practicing had been a great source of spiritual nurture. With two small children, she realized that not only had she given up practicing the piano; she had also given up a source of spiritual nurture. She recognized that to make a commitment to an hour of practice a day (a former pattern of hers) was simply out of the question. She felt, however, that fifteen minutes twice a week was possible. She picked a goal that was small and yet offered an opportunity to engage intentionally in spiritual growth.

Instructions for Making a Rule of Life

1. Invite people to list the things they do to nourish or "give life" to their spirits. Ask about their "spirits" rather than their "spiritual lives" in order not to restrict their imaginations to only their religious practices. Asking specifically about spiritual life may limit the scope of the answers to activities associated with religious practices and thereby eliminate one of the primary purposes of making the Rule.

2. Ask those who are willing to share something from their lists. Let the group get a sense of the wide variety of practices people use to nurture their spirits. This may help people discover additional ways to celebrate and develop their spirituality.

3. Ask the group: What do you notice about your list? Are there surprises? Is there something on your list you did not expect? Is there something you notice you did not include? By looking over their lists, many people discover things previously unrealized; for example, a meaningful activity they already do may have spiritual significance they had not recognized.

4. Explain how the list can also be used for personal growth. Ask the group: Is there anything you would like to add, or do more frequently, or remove from your list? How will doing this assist in your spiritual growth? Are you certain your growth step is very small? As a spiritual leader you can help people be realistic about appropriate growth and God's steady, gentle call.

Individual and Group Use

Hearing what nurtures other people's spirits is itself enriching for the entire group. It helps people discover the many ways God is at work in people's lives, and it gives new ideas for spiritual nurture. Those who do this privately can easily follow the steps of the exercise. Although they miss the sharing, working on their Rule of Life nevertheless affirms the practices and means used to sustain their spirit and provides a pathway for continued growth.

FOUR-STRANDED GARLAND

Background

The Four-Stranded Garland is a method of prayer recommended by Martin Luther (1483–1546). Luther, well known for his desire to reform the Roman Catholic Church, is reported by his colleague Melanchthon to have nailed his Ninety-Five Theses to the door of Wittenberg Church on October 31, 1517.[4] His concerns regarding ecclesiastical and doctrinal reform (discussed in Chapter 1) often eclipse our awareness of his understanding of spiritual practices, including prayer. The prayer recommended by Luther in 1535—the Four-Stranded Garland— seems clearly to reflect prayer practices he would have learned as a younger man.

In 1506 Luther became an Augustinian monk. As an ordained Augustinian monk, Luther also would have learned the practice of sacred reading (*Lectio Divina*) or, as it is sometimes called today, praying with Scripture. In this form of prayer one sits quietly with a text, gently listening both for the meaning and the affective impact conveyed by the words. Through this quiet, reflective process the richness of the text is allowed to speak. At the same time, the text becomes internalized in the person praying.

The Augustinians recognized Luther's potential as a scholar and in 1513 placed him in a teaching position at the recently founded University of Wittenberg. Here Luther began teaching Scripture studies. During these early years he produced extensive lectures on biblical texts, including the Psalms, Galatians, Hebrews, and Romans.

Luther's scholarly life within a religious community insured that he was well schooled both in the study of Scripture and in the faithful exercise of prayer. It seems apparent that Luther's own experience of "justification not by works, but by faith" grew out of his devotional wrestling with Paul's letter to the Romans. As detailed in Chapter 1, Luther's experience of wrestling with the Romans 1:16–17 text led to a breakthrough in his understanding of God: God was no longer a frightful judge who delighted in sending sinners to hell, but a loving God whose mercy was extended to people of faith. Believers needed to trust, not fear, God.

This insight brought Luther an accompanying sense of relief. The fears of former days were diminished, and his new relationship with God was grounded in trust and love. In the context of this new relationship, Luther could confess his sins without the fear of being sent to hell and could trust that God would continue to guide his daily life. In the dynamics of this breakthrough event we see four moments: (1) instruction from the Scripture (justification by faith, not works); (2) thanksgiving (for the gift of grace offered by God to believers); (3) confession (claiming one's sins without fear of hell); (4) guidance (the trust that God will continue to provide daily guidance). This pattern became the method of prayer recommended by Luther to Peter his barber.

In a work titled *A Simple Way to Pray*,[5] Luther describes the movement in prayer as a four-stranded garland. Weaving together these four strands corresponds to the movements noted above: instruction, thanksgiving, confession, guidance. As a prayer method, it assumes a devotional approach to the text; yet the one praying begins with an awareness that the text offers instruction that may be informed by scholarly study.

Luther believed that this method could be used both with Scripture texts and with other historic statements of faith. For example, he recommended using it on a frequent basis with the Ten Commandments as well as with the Apostles' Creed. In each case the prayer time is shaped by an internal dialogue that ponders over the sacred texts. This dialogue, however, at the point of prayer is not a detached discussion of the meaning of the text. It is rather an experience of finding the meaning of the text for one's personal life. Through this process Luther believed we deepen our relationship with God and gain guidance for living a faithful life.

Use of the Practice

Mainline Protestants have traditionally approached the biblical texts with a desire to know and understand the teachings contained therein. The Protestant emphasis on the Word has made Bible study a staple of Protestant denominations since the Reformation. Although such study may or may not be informed by the methods of biblical criticism taught in most mainline

Protestant seminaries, the Bible itself is nevertheless an object
of study. Devotional uses of the text usually involve applying
the insights of a passage to one's life or in some instances mem-
orizing familiar passages. The method contained in the Four-
Stranded Garland begins with a focus on instruction, but
requires that participants move beyond the knowledge base of
the instruction to its affective implications for daily life.
This involves reading the Scripture passage, creed, or other
sacred text five times. Each reading should be performed by a
different group member. People report that hearing the passage
in different voices with different emphases on particular words
contributes to the significance of the experience. The first reading should be rendered at a regular pace while participants are
invited to listen for the overall sense of the passage. The second through the fifth readings should be performed slowly. The
purpose of these readings is to allow the participants to pon-
der the text, allowing it to touch the deeper parts of the human
soul. For most mainline Protestants, this type of listening will
need to be learned. Distinguishing the knowledge-based approach of Bible study from the devotional expectations of this
method will help participants grasp the difference.

Between the second through the fifth readings, participants
are also invited to share a word or phrase with the group that
expresses their respective reactions to instruction, thanksgiving, confession, and guidance. Here again mainline Protestants
will have a tendency to move from a mood of prayer to that of
study and discussion. Invite people to share a word, phrase, or
idea, but not to engage in discussion or elaborate on their concern. Group members are asked to listen prayerfully, but not
comment on the reflections of others. Leaders may want to
demonstrate both the pace of the slow readings as well as an
example of sharing a word, phrase, or idea without further
elaboration or discussion.

Leaders need to be patient. Learning to listen to texts devotionally and share in accordance with the method requires
skill. Most mainline Protestants have not been exposed to these
skills. Remember, too, that people engage texts as they are able.
God is working even in groups that have difficulty learning
these devotional skills.

Affirming the importance of critical reflection on the biblical texts will be important. Mainline Protestants may at first fear that this devotional approach is asking them to disregard their biblical knowledge; for example, the historical context of the passage, the intent of the biblical authors; the social location of contemporary readers. Luther's method does not ask that these items be discounted; it merely acknowledges that a devotional stance involves a different method that is also a legitimate approach to the text.

Texts are often selected from the lectionary readings for the upcoming Sunday. The leader needs to choose a text that is sufficiently long to provide a variety of participants ample material, yet not so long that the readings become distracting or exhausting. Readings the length of the Twenty-third Psalm are appropriate. This may require using only selected verses from the lectionary options.

Instructions for the Leader

Select a Scripture passage or other devotional reading, and provide the group with Bibles or a printed text. Invite the group to sit quietly and take a few moments to center themselves. Ask them to get in touch with what they are feeling. To prepare for prayer, invite people to turn over to God any concerns or feelings that may be distracting, knowing that God's compassion is all embracing.

Instructions for the Participants

1. *First reading of Scripture:* Listen quietly to the text for an overall sense of its meaning.

2. *Second reading:* Listen as the text is read more slowly. Listen for the word, phrase, or idea that comes to you as a word of instruction. After the reading, pause for a time of silence.

3. Invite those who are comfortable to share by speaking the word, phrase, or idea that came as a word in instruction.

4. *Third reading:* Attend to the word, image, or phrase of the text that came to you as a word of instruction. As you hear

the passage this time, allow yourself to feel a sense of gratitude for the instruction that has come to you. Give yourself permission to feel this gratitude deeply. Allow a time of silence after the reading.

5. Invite the group to share the word, phrase, or image that came with a sense of gratitude.

6. *Fourth reading:* As you listen to the reading of the text, listen for the word, phrase, or image that calls you to confession. Allow yourself to feel appropriate sorrow for that which you need to confess. Allow a time of silence after the reading.

7. Invite participants to share the word, phrase, or image that prompted their confession. (Leaders need to be aware that people may not want to share if the issues that emerge are highly personal and sufficient trust has yet to develop in the group.)

8. *Fifth reading:* As you listen again to the text, contemplate the way God is guiding you in the words or phrases to which you have been attending. Rest in the feeling that is indeed leading you, even if you are not certain about the direction. Allow a period of silence following the reading.

9. If the group feels comfortable to do so, have them share how God is present to them.

10. If others have shared words, phrases, or thoughts that have deepened their own sense of God's working in their life and they want to share these with the group, have them do so now.

11. After the sharing has been completed, allow time to experience a sense of gratitude for this time to be together in God's presence. Savor the silence.

12. Close with a spoken or silent prayer of thanksgiving.

Individual and Group Use

The Four-Stranded Garland can also be used as a prayer method by those praying alone. Follow the steps above. The readings may be performed either silently or aloud. Hearing the readings read aloud in your own voice may add depth to the experience. People frequently report that reading a passage aloud opens up insights and feelings not tapped as readily by silent reading. When you come to the time for sharing, say your word or phrase out loud. Hearing the word or phrase spoken aloud in your own voice allows you to experience and encounter the word. Giving voice to the word can contribute to the depth of your encounter with the text.

PRAYER OF EXAMEN

Background

In *Institutes of the Christian Religion,* John Calvin (1509–1564) calls prayer "the chief exercise of faith" and speaks at considerable length about its nature and importance. Speaking of the necessity of prayer, Calvin says that in prayer God is made present to believers. It is through prayer that we are reminded that our daily benefits come from God. Prayer is an activity that keeps the heart burning with the desire "to seek, love, and serve" God.[6]

By praying we enter into conversation with God. According to Calvin, to enter this conversation we need to observe four rules for prayer.[7] First, we need to acquire an attitude of "devout detachment." This requires clearing the mind of any thoughts that would lead it "away from right and pure contemplation of God." Being freed of distracting and wandering thoughts permits the mind to rise above itself. Calvin acknowledges that we cannot always be freed from our anxieties—nor should we—but we should strive for a level of concentration that opens us to awe and reverence. Second, persons must pray with a sincere desire for prayer and with humility. Calvin notes specifically the need to avoid using prayers in a perfunctory fashion, for example, intoning prayers by rote or mumbling prayers. Such prayer is indicative of a cold heart. Third, we must stand before God in humility and offer our confessions. Prayers are offered to God not as testimonies to human righteousness, but as pleas for God's mercy. Asking for the forgiveness of sins is, according to Calvin, the most important part of prayer. This involves taking "account each day of recent sins." Recognizing our propensity to sin reminds us that we constantly stand in need of God's mercy and grace. Fourth, when we pray with true humility we have confident hope that such prayers will be answered. This assurance that God does indeed answer prayer does not bring with it a "sweet and perfect repose" that releases one from all anxiety. Calvin observes that those who seek such comforts generally lack the sense of caring that motivates faithful actions. The saints, he notes, are troubled by the problems that surround them, are motivated to address these problems, yet also take refuge in God, knowing that God is ready to extend a helping hand.

Calvin's spirituality affirms the centrality of the mystical union between the believer and Christ. The indwelling of Christ in the hearts of believers makes them sharers of his gifts.[8] As a result, believers—who are "engrafted" into the body of Christ—find Christ not by looking outward but by looking within. It is this indwelling of Christ that makes it possible for the faithful to grow into the "likeness" of Christ. This growth does not suggest that the believer becomes God by uniting with Christ. Christ and the believer are not of the same essence or substance. The believer's will, however, is capable of growing more fully into the likeness of Christ. This opportunity for spiritual growth gave people in the Reformed traditions an identifiable role for sanctification (discussed in Chapter 1) that was missing from Luther's selective focus on justification by faith. Calvin believed that persons could with the aid of grace become more Christlike. Calvin affirmed the significance of justification by faith, but he also believed this faith would produce in the lives of believers a desire to grow in faith and a desire to live a holy life filled with acts of love and service.

Many people in mainline Protestant denominations have (for reasons discussed in Chapter 1) been unaware of Protestant teachings on prayer. For many, discovering Calvin's teachings on prayer brings joy. Learning that Calvin understood prayer as the "chief exercise of faith" and that he located the heart as the center of prayer gives a sensitivity to Calvin's theology that many Protestants have missed. Moreover, from his rules regarding prayer it seems clear that Calvin himself engaged in what we today might call centering prayer. His starting point for prayer—the mystical union between the believer and Christ—also reminds us that the deeply experienced insights of contemplation were not alien to Calvin's experiences. It is somewhat ironic that although Calvin did not encourage mystical prayer, his own understanding of prayer begins with the mystical union between Christ and the believer.

The Prayer of Examen that follows represents an attempt to be faithful to Calvin's commitments to a life of service and to his rules for prayer. It provides a framework for exploring God's involvement in daily life.

Use of the Practice

A Prayer of Examen is used to reflect on the nature of God's activity in human life. These prayer forms—found in several faith traditions—were used by the desert fathers and mothers to deepen their relationship with God. I have composed the prayer used here based on other prayers of examen,[9] but with the intent of reflecting Calvin's belief that we can locate God's activity in our daily life of work and service. Calvin contended that people need to reflect their God-given grace in lives of Christian love and service. This prayer is intended to help people discern where God is working in their lives, especially in the call to service.

A Prayer of Examen involves two major activities: (1) an examination of consciousness to discover how God has been present throughout our day; (2) an examination of conscience to discover those areas in our lives that need further growth and healing. The Psalmist says in Psalm 139:1: "O LORD, you have searched me and known me." A Prayer of Examen helps us search ourselves for an awareness of God's presence in ordinary events. It helps us see how our thoughts, feelings, and actions can more faithfully serve God's work in our daily lives.

Instructions for Prayer

1. Quiet yourself. Remember that in prayer you are entering into a relationship with God. Using whatever method you

find most helpful, take a few moments to move beyond whatever may distract you or intrude on your quiet. Gently find the still point within your being.

2. Allow yourself time to appreciate the silence. Invite God to be present with you in this time of prayer.

3. Now look back over the past twenty-four hours. Beginning with the present moment, let each hour of the past day gently pass by your awareness. (For the purposes of the exercise, I will arbitrarily assume you are doing this at 2 P.M. When using the exercise, begin at the point in the day when you are teaching it. Pause between each question.) Notice what you are doing now. What were you doing just before coming here? Where did you have lunch? With whom did you have lunch? What were you doing before lunch? What were you doing during the morning hours? What did you do after breakfast? What was breakfast like this morning? Where did you eat? Whom were you with? What did you do before breakfast? Did you have a restful or interrupted night's sleep? Did you dream? When did you go to bed last night? How did you spend your evening? With whom did you have dinner? What were you doing before dinner? How did you spend your afternoon after 2 P.M.?

4. What are you noticing that you have taken for granted during the past twenty-four hours of your life? What feelings and thoughts are emerging as you look back over the past twenty-four hours?

5. Now look back again over this period of time and reflect on the way in which God has been present in your life. Where do you see God at work in your life in the past twenty-four hours? In joys, fears, suffering, work? In an act of service? In your reading? In an event, person, sound, nature, music, action?

6. When in the past twenty-four hours did you feel you were cooperating most fully with God's action in your life?

7. Are there areas of your life where you feel you were resisting God's presence or not listening carefully enough to God's

will? Are there actions or thoughts that require God's pardon? The pardon of others?

8. In what ways do you believe God may be calling you to a new awareness, a change of heart, to different actions?

9. Do you have a sense of gratitude for one or two particular ways that God was present in your life during the past twenty-four hours? If so, allow yourself to experience deeply this sense of thankfulness. Depending on what is appropriate for your context or situation, express your feelings silently or aloud, using words, movement, or journal keeping.

10. Conclude this period of prayer with a time of silence.

11. At the conclusion of your prayer time, reflect for a few moments on what you have observed about how God is working in your daily life. Do any of these insights need to be followed by actions? Write, perhaps in a journal, things to which you may want to return.

Individual and Group Use

The Prayer of Examen can be used by both groups and individuals. People attending retreats or other church-related programs often find the experience of examen helpful. It can also be a helpful addition to church meetings. In such cases the participants may want to look back on how God has been at work in their monthly or quarterly gatherings. People can be asked to reflect on how God has been at work in their corporate life. Committees can be asked if they feel they are cooperating with God's work in the life of the church. How might they be resisting? What are they being called to do as a committee?

People who want to include this exercise as a regular part of their spiritual practice must decide the frequency with which they want to do it: daily, weekly, or monthly. If one records at regular intervals any of the observations or insights that emerge from the practice, it may be useful to review these notes on a monthly basis to see if any patterns emerge. It is not unusual to find that at particular times in our lives God's activity may be discerned in patterns we can discover. Through this process it is also possible to discern obstacles hindering spiritual growth.

Prayer for a New Earth

Background

This Prayer for a New Earth embodies both the historic Protestant emphasis on living a socially responsible life and the recent efforts by many mainline Protestants to transcend the false dichotomy between prayer and social action. Although mainline Protestant denominations have frequently challenged their members to adopt prophetic stands on a variety of crucial social issues, little has been done specifically in the area of spiritual nurture.

Today, however, there is a growing recognition that nurturing the spiritual life is not antithetical to commitments in the arena of peace and justice. For example, mainline Protestants have increasingly understood that the Roman Catholic Church fosters in its members a commitment both to the ongoing work for justice/peace and to prayer/reflection. Arguments that people of prayer are simply "navel gazing" and that people working for justice are "working out unresolved personal anger" are recognized as illegitimate. Narcissism and unresolved anger may be present in some acts of prayer or justice, but that does not warrant dismissing the legitimate religious needs to nurture one's spirit and act in behalf of peace and justice. I wonder, too, if you have noticed that God sometimes uses narcissistic and angry people for holy purposes!

There is also an increasing recognition that contemplative and meditative practices that foster spiritual growth are as important for laity as for professional religious leaders. The Protestant reformers of the sixteenth century contended that a call to a secular vocation (a job in the world) could be as meaningful as a call to a religious vocation. Until the Reformation, religious vocations were generally deemed more worthwhile than secular jobs. The broader understanding of vocation, however, did not break down the barriers that existed between the prayer practices considered suitable for the vowed religious (priests, nuns, and brothers) and those offered to the laity. It was not until the post–Vatican II emphasis on "the people of God" that Roman Catholic retreat houses opened their doors widely both to their own laity and to Protestants. An aspect of the current enthusiasm for spiritual renewal grows from the realization that spiritual practices can helpfully inform and bless the lives of those both inside and outside religious vocations and orders.

Use of the Practice

This prayer practice is designed to reflect the Protestant belief that God's work occurs in all venues of life. God is at work in our personal lives, our social relationships, our homes, our places of work, and in the realm of nature. Those seeking to grow spiritually need to look intentionally for God's activity in all aspects of life and align themselves with that work. The prophet Micah (6:8) reminds us that doing justice is as important as showing lovingkindness and walking humbly with God. Frequently, however, it is not easy to discern the forces of justice, compassion, peace, and hope in our midst. Other forces such as greed, racism, consumerism, nationalism, and sexism vie for our allegiance. They encourage us to see the world from their respective positions. Nourishing the spiritual life is a means of keeping our spirits and actions attuned to God's leading.

Instructions for Prayer

This exercise in reflective prayer is intended to increase your awareness of God's activity in the world you inhabit. It is not intended as a time of intercessory prayer for the people and situations upon which you will be asked to reflect. In this exercise you are looking for the concerns and issues that require attention. Some may be significant because of their emotional salience; others because an issue or concern needs immediate attention. Others may be more subtle and noticeable because of the persistence of God's gentle nudge.

1. Take time to quiet yourself. Notice how you are feeling. Are you sitting in a comfortable position? If you need to move

around to be comfortable, do that now. If you are not already
doing so, you may want to close your eyes. Slowly take and
release one or two deep breaths.

2. If you are feeling relaxed and receptive, invite God to be with
you as you enter this time of reflection. Remember that God
is always as near to us as our breath.

3. Take a few moments and visualize your home; now visualize the people who live with you in your home.

   a. Where do you see God at work in your home life? What
   is the source of compassion in your home? Justice? Love?
   Hope? Who in your home is striving to support these
   forces? Do the people in your home share these commitments? What are the major issues at the present time in
   your household? How is God present or absent in these
   issues? Is there anything you need to do or stop doing to
   be aligned with the work of God in your home? Is there
   a way you need to support more fully God's work in the
   lives of those in your home?

   b. If something significant has emerged as you have taken
   inventory of the movement of God's activity in your home
   and you would like to make a note of it in your journal,
   take a few moments and do so now.

4. If you are ready to move on, take a few moments and visualize your workplace—your office or the space where you
work.

   a. Where do you see God's activity in your workplace? Is
   there a place you feel God's concerns are being overlooked
   or dismissed? Imagine the faces of the people with whom
   you work. Do you have a sense that their actions are sup-
   porting justice, equity, compassion, and hope? What are
   the major issues currently requiring attention in your
   workplace? Is there a sense that God's activity is present
   in any of these issues? Are there neglected concerns that
   should receive attention? Are there other issues that require resolution? If so, will you have any opportunity to
   align yourself with what you feel is God's activity in the

setting? Are there informal things you need to do—or not do? Are there formal actions you need to take—or thwart?

b. If something from your inventory of your workplace suggests things you need to remember, please take time now to note your concerns.

5. Now direct your attention to your community. (You may invite people to visualize their local community or a wider area, for example, a state/province or the nation.)

a. What are the major issues at the present time in your community? Have you thought about what God's will might be toward these issues? Can you sense where the work of justice, compassion, or hope exists in these community issues? Is there something you feel called to do in support of God's work in the community? What follow-up do you need to do in response to God's call? Is there a person with whom you should speak? Are there specific actions you should take?

b. If you have become aware of some actions or thoughts that you want to remember, please take a few moments to record them now.

6. Now visualize the planet earth. In your imagination, picture planet earth in the solar system, one small object in the midst of infinite space.

a. As you think of planet earth, visualize the patchwork of boundary lines that demarcate various countries. Are there areas of the globe where you believe God's compassion and justice are especially needed? Which areas come to your mind? Are there conflicts that need to be settled? People who need to be fed? Naked who need clothing? Prisoners requiring visitation? Now ask yourself if there is anything you need to do to support God's efforts to address or alleviate these needs? Is there any action to which you feel called? If so, what will it require of you? When will you do it? Do you need to set a time now?

b. Take a few moments to note anything you feel called to do in response to these needs.

c. Now visualize the globe without the geographic bound-aries. Visualize the mountains and rivers, the deserts and plains; visualize the birds of the air; the animals of the forests, the fish of the sea. In your imagination visualize the polar ice caps and the heat of the rain forests. As you use your mind's eye to take in this vast and complex panorama, imagine some of the places where God is at work. What do you understand is the work of God in re-gard to this creation? Is there something you need to do locally to support God's desires for the planet? A cause you need to support? A local cause or an international cause? A contribution you want to make? Is there some-thing else you need to do to support God's care for the planet?

d. Take a moment to record your concerns that require follow-up.

7. Now take a moment and reflect on the various ways God is at work in the world. Take time to consider where you are being called in the midst of all these concerns. No one can do everything. Almost everyone can do something. Lis-ten quietly to God's voice within you as you look back over your jottings to see what needs immediate attention. Listen in the quiet for guidance in prioritizing your list. Note any-thing that emerges.

8. Once you have established some priority for your list, take a few moments in the quiet and give thanks for the oppor-tunity to serve the God who loves you, the God who is closer to you than your own heartbeat.

9. If you are doing this in a group, come back to this space and this time. Stretch or move about as you need.

10. Allow time for group sharing about the experience. Was the exercise helpful? In what way? What was not helpful? Were there any new insights about God's activity? Were there any new insights about your personal actions or responsibilities?

Individual and Group Use

The exercise can be used either in groups or by individuals. The group sharing at the end often helps consolidate what is learned and frequently is a source of enrichment.

MORNING AND EVENING PRAYER

Background

Morning and evening prayer services in the Protestant church traditions owe their origins to the services of prayer established by the Roman Catholic breviary—the worship book containing prayers, services, and hymns. As discussed earlier, the attempt to "pray without ceasing" encouraged by the apostle Paul inspired those living religious lives to pray corporately throughout the day. The number of services was influenced by Psalm 119:164: "Seven times a day I praise you." Although the prayer services evolved over time, it is likely a roster of prayer services was established by the end of the fifth century. By the sixteenth century the number of religious festivals, special days honoring saints, and prayers for the dead had complicated the structure of these services. Reform was needed. The Roman Catholic Church in the Western world responded by establishing seven services for prayer: Matins and Yauds (treated as one—held sometime between midnight to 2 A.M.), Prime (6 A.M.), Terce (9 A.M.), Sext (Noon), None (3 P.M.), Vespers (evening), Compline (just before bed).

In the Protestant traditions, these services and their times were either greatly amended (for example, Anglican and Lutheran traditions) or they fell into disuse as regular occasions for public worship (for example, the United Presbyterian Church or the United Church of Christ). The worship or service books that most mainline Protestant traditions provide still contain services for morning and evening prayer. Many of their elements are taken from the Protestant reforms initiated at the time of the Reformation.

In the Lutheran tradition, morning and evening prayer services in the language of the people (rather than Latin) drew on elements from their Roman Catholic predecessors. Morning prayer used for Sunday services and special religious festivals combined elements of matins and lauds. The evening prayer service was influenced primarily by vespers. In each case, however, there was a shift from the Roman Catholic focus on the reading of the psalms to a new emphasis on longer portions of other Scriptures. The Protestant emphasis on the proclaimed Word is seen here in the insistence that morning and evening prayer services include the preaching of a sermon.

In the Anglican tradition, a more complex fusion of the earlier Roman Catholic services produced an order for morning and evening prayer that differed from their Lutheran counterparts. Thomas Cranmer (1489–1556), Archbishop of Canterbury (1533–1556), had followed closely the developments in Germany as the Reformation spread by participating in a group of English scholars known as "Little Germany." When Cranmer wrote the 1552 edition of *The Book of Common Prayer*, he created, following the continental reforms, two offices—morning and evening prayer. His liturgical genius, however, fused elements of the Roman Catholic services of matins, lauds, and prime to make the English matins or morning service. For the English evensong service, he brought together elements of vespers and compline. In this way Cranmer created two offices, using key elements from five of the eight pre-Reformation services.[10]

Today a number of people are rediscovering the spiritual value of participating in morning and/or evening prayer as a spiritual discipline. Participants note that practicing morning or evening prayer services provides an external structure to their spiritual lives that they find helpful in maintaining the discipline of regular attendance. For many people it is also significant that they are hearing Scriptures, praying prayers, and joining in the reading of psalms that are being used throughout the day by others from around the world. The phenomenon of raising a "single" plea from many voices is a way of affirming one's unity with others around the world.

Participation in morning and/or evening prayer can be accomplished in a number of ways. People who live near mainline Protestant churches or cathedrals of the more liturgically formal denominations, such as Lutheran or Anglican traditions, may be able to attend an established public service. Some years ago I knew a man who throughout his life had served the church as a layperson. He said that in retirement one of his wishes was to live near a large liturgically formal church so that he could participate in both morning and evening prayer on a daily basis. Although his wife felt no calling to this daily discipline, she supported his efforts for relocation. The last I heard, he had been attending morning and evening prayer on a daily basis (except when they were out of town) for more than five years!

Many of us do not reside near a cathedral or church offering such opportunities. Others may have occupational or personal demands that preclude such involvement. Small-group formats, however, provide another way for engaging in these services. Morning and evening prayer rituals normally do not require the presence of clergy. Small prayer groups or study groups can easily use the service book of their particular denomination and together provide the leadership for these services. Lectionaries provide a list of Scripture readings that are suitable throughout the church year.

A third option is to follow the daily office of morning and/or evening prayer as a solitary act of devotion. In addition to the services that are provided in the denominational manuals (books of order, common prayer, and worship), there are other devotional resources that provide orders for morning and evening prayer. Although some of these are easily acquired books or booklets of devotions, others are offered as guides for a particular denomination. For example, the United Church Press (United Church of Christ press) has for the past few years published *The Book of Daily Prayer: Morning and Evening*. This resource provides Scripture readings and prayers for each day of the year.

KEEPING A JOURNAL

Background

In the Protestant tradition, journal keeping gained special importance in the lives of English and American Puritans. The journals of Quakers such as George Fox (1624–1691) and John

Woolman (1720–1972) record not only important events in their daily lives, but the religious significance of these events. Woolman, whose commitment to the abolition of slavery was a major thrust of his religious message, tells in his journal of the importance of God's presence in his life. Reading the personal reflections found in journal entries provides a glimpse of God's activity in the lives of the faithful, and opens new insights into the depths of turmoil, grief, and despair as well as hope, meaning, and joy that filled these lives.

Keeping a journal is also beneficial for us today. The recording of our thoughts, longings, dreams, and hopes often makes these intangibles more accessible. For some people journals contain an account of significant life events and their reactions to them. Others find journals especially significant for psychological or spiritual development. Seeing our inner life displayed on a page provides an opportunity for a deeper encounter with its rich texture.

Although precise definitions of journals vary, there are distinguishing marks that differentiate journals according to purpose and style. Although the word *diary* is listed in *The American Heritage Dictionary*[11] as a synonym for journal, in contemporary usage a diary is often associated with a recording of events rather than with reflection on them. Many people who keep diaries list the significant events of a day or week without providing much personal reflection on the events. The word *journal*, as it is used today, generally connotes written reflections on some significant aspect of one's life.

Often people associate journals with the approach established by Ira Progoff.[12] He encouraged people to dialogue in their journals with parents, dreams, significant past events, or any emotionally significant material that emerged from their conscious or unconscious life. People who learned this technique for keeping a journal used it as a means to grow emotionally and often spiritually. The focus, however, remained predominantly on psychological growth.

Journals may also be kept as a means to foster our spiritual development. In contrast to the approach that focuses primarily on personal integration and growth, the spiritual journal explores life from the perspective of the holy. Where is

God at work in my life today? How do I understand God's call in the present moment? Where is God leading me at this time? How have I fallen short? Are there things I can do to cooperate more fully with God's work in my life? The dialogue that emerges from these questions and from encounters with the holy provides the content for the spiritual journal. Much of the material that emerges may reflect both spiritual and psychological insights. In this sense a spiritual journal will have things in common with psychologically focused journals, but a spiritual journal will intentionally relate the material that emerges in a life of faith.

People keeping spiritual journals may focus explicitly on the day's or week's events and record how they understand God to be present there. Many record things that emerge in prayer or as a result of involvement with other spiritual practices. Sometimes these are small insights about a specific concern; at other times they may be profound encounters with the holy. In either case the journal functions like a testament or a book of the Bible: It is a record of an individual's encounter with God. Some people carefully record many details; others record only things that shape or contribute to the "big" picture. No single style is "right." We must discover, individually, the form of journaling that personally suits our needs. The purpose of keeping a journal is to make us more aware of God's presence in our lives and of ways we can participate more fully in the work of God.

Instructions for Getting Started

The instructions provided here are specifically for keeping a journal designed for spiritual growth.

1. Decide if you want to try keeping a journal as a practice designed for spiritual growth. You may want to experiment with this for a few days or weeks. Write down significant events, prayers, conversations, dreams, memories, or any other encounter that seems related to your spiritual growth. After a few days ask yourself if this activity seems helpful or meaningful. Is this something to which you can commit yourself? If you have a regular prayer practice, does writing in the journal after prayer seem helpful? If the answer to

these questions is yes, you may want to explore using a form of journal keeping as a means for spiritual growth.

2. Buy an attractive but inexpensive book or notebook for recording your material. For many people, having a religious symbol or motif (for example, dancing figures) on their journal cover reminds them of the sacred nature of keeping a journal for spiritual growth.

3. Consider how often you are going to write in your journal. Frequency is an important issue: Are you going to write in your journal daily, weekly, or monthly? Perhaps you are going to record only major events or significant encounters. Will you plan to write after times of prayer? If that is your intent, keep your journal near your place of prayer. Do you plan to write in the morning or the evening? When can you find quiet time for reflection and writing? Where will you do your writing? In your home or at the office? Experiment with these factors, but recognize that until you establish some type of routine your journal keeping will probably not be as helpful as it might be otherwise.

4. After a week of writing and then again after a month of writing, reread everything that you have recorded. Examine the material to see if God has been at work in your life in ways you did not notice until now. Are there any patterns? Any common themes? Are there ways God has been trying to get your attention that you have ignored or overlooked? Does anything concerning your relationship with the sacred emerge?

5. If you have a spiritual director or a group where personal issues are shared, you may want to share some of your insights, questions, frustrations, and joys that emerge from your journal keeping.

6. If journal keeping is helpful, save your journals. They are your personal record of your encounter with the holy. At times in your life when you are in turmoil or your prayer life seems endlessly dry, you may find it meaningful to reread your journals. The purpose of rereading is not to try to

"manufacture" encounters with God that are joyful, but to recognize that most people have periods that are dry and others that are fruitful. Notice that in this regard your journey parallels the joys and trials of many biblical figures, including the Psalmist, Job, and Jesus.

COVENANT GROUP

Background

John Wesley (1703–1791) and his brother Charles (1707–1788) were sons of an Anglican cleric. John Wesley believed that once a person experienced "justification by faith," something was done not only *for* believers but *in* believers. That is, God not only extended mercy for the believer's salvation; God also gave the gift of the Spirit. With the cooperation of the newly born Spirit within, believers continue the journey toward perfection or holiness. Thus, in Wesley's theology, sanctification, or growth in holiness, is central to spiritual development. As with the Pietists (discussed in Chapter 1), Wesley's understanding of perfection did not imply that humans were free from committing errors. Instead, perfection referred to the spiritual growth that the indwelling Spirit made possible: Human intentions could be increasingly purified, thus permitting persons to grow in love and avoid conscious acts of sin. Although Wesley did contend that a person could at least in theory achieve entire sanctification—including the freedom from sin—he noted that he had never met a person so blessed.

Spiritual growth required the use of spiritual disciplines, a commitment to the Eucharist, and acts of compassionate social responsibility. By committing oneself to spiritual disciplines, one's human will is brought into conformity with God's will. Wesley recognized that furthering this spiritual development required not only a commitment to individual exercises and actions, but the support and accountability provided by small groups. At Oxford in 1729, a small covenant group, called a Holy Club, was organized by Charles and led by John. Members of the Holy Club were committed to the daily office, daily self-examination, Bible study, penance and fasting, twice-weekly celebration of the Eucharist, and works of mercy among the poor. These guidelines for Christian living provided the necessary structure for living the commitments of the group on a daily basis. Growth in prayer and service emerged from the desire to give one's life to God and God's purposes. By meeting with one another on a scheduled basis, the members had a forum for accountability, mutual support, and confession.

This so-called methodical approach to spiritual development was ridiculed by some members of the university community. As a sign of derision, they called the Wesleys and their followers Methodists. Although both John and Charles Wesley died Anglicans, John's understanding of spiritual development and his commitment to covenant groups provided the vision that eventually led to the establishment of the Methodist Church.

Instructions for Designing a Group Covenant

Those who decide to participate in a small group committed to spiritual development may want to create a group covenant that will give guidance and direction to their growth. Often groups decide to be accountable to each other by sharing their faith and by sharing their personal growth on a regular basis. Groups may also covenant to work on goals shared by all members of the group. Following Wesley's concern for spiritual development through prayer, worship, and action, members of the group may want to have a personal sharing time (check-in), joint worship and prayer, and a commitment to action in behalf of those in need. Normally such groups would meet for 1 or 1½ hours either weekly or monthly.

Group members who have used the Rule of Life exercise can use it as a basis for negotiating a small-group covenant with others. By sharing with one another what each one does to nourish spiritual development, group members can discover what they share in common. Such sharing will contribute to building a consensus around the activities to be engaged in by all group members. The covenant can also be designed to accommodate individual needs and goals. A sample of a group covenant and a sample of an individual covenant follow. These are intended simply as examples and are not intended to promote any particular types of spiritual practices or activities.

Group Covenant for Faithful Living

Group Time

1. We will check in with each other each time we meet in order to share important joys or concerns in our lives since the last meeting.

2. We will share a time of prayer together. (This can take different forms or follow a set form.)

3. We will discuss and establish long-term and short-term goals for spiritual growth.

4. We will share how we are doing with our goals, celebrating together our successes and confessing our failures.

5. We will have a service project as part of our outreach. (This can be any project decided upon by the members of the group. Examples of projects include doing things for the needy, writing letters for Amnesty International, working on environmental concerns.)

6. We will support each member as he or she develops personal goals and activities not shared by the entire group.

Individual Covenant for Personal Time

Some members may have, in addition to the group covenant, other activities, practices, or commitments to which they would like to be held individually accountable and for which they would appreciate receiving support. The individual covenant would include only activities the members did not covenant to do as a group.[13]

1. I will engage in twenty minutes of prayer each day.

2. I will attend church weekly.

3. I will nurture my spirit by walking regularly in a natural setting.

4. I will seek to be more patient in my home.

5. I will do Bible reading at home three times a week.

6. I will work at my church on the Outreach Committee.

7. I will contribute to an environmental cause.

8. I will work to become more aware of God's presence in my daily life.

9. I will do volunteer work at a hospital.

10. I will listen more carefully to my family (or co-workers, and so forth).

Individual and Group Use

Although it may not be possible to form a small covenant group that meets face-to-face for support and accountability, in the contemporary context other options exist. I have known groups of clergy who decided to establish covenant groups during continuing education events. Although in many cases travel costs and distance would prohibit future meetings, they decided to hold each other accountable through conference telephone calls. I know of groups who decided to use the Internet or E-mail as a means of keeping in touch.

Individual covenants, of course, have spiritual significance even if not shared with a small group. They help us see what we actually plan to do; this often differs from the understanding we carry around in our heads of what we "plan" to do. Putting the covenant on paper gives it a status and reality that it does not otherwise acquire. It also helps people be realistic about their own personal expectations and goals. Some individuals choose to share their covenants with their spiritual directors as a means of support and accountability.

Conclusion

The spiritual exercises provided in this book are resources for individuals and faith communities struggling to discern God's leading in an individualistic, consumer-oriented society. Faithfulness—the ongoing desire to follow God's leading—is foolishness in the eyes of a society that rewards the best, the rich, and the famous. Although the society around us encourages us to follow paths that lead to success, following God's calling more often entails being asked to embrace a cross.

Being faithful means that we listen for God's leading above all else, that we embark on a risky journey. We struggle to be faithful, to be disciplined in prayer and just in our actions. Yet like our biblical ancestors we turn away from God in spite of our best intentions. We are seduced by consumerism, manipulated by those who value what we produce and not who we are, and we get caught in the fantasy that we are self-made people. God, however, is a gracious God who knows that we make mistakes and who offers us new opportunities to listen and return to the path.

Those who seek God's way continually discover that the spiritual journey is our only deeply meaningful option. It is the journey home.

Our own Protestant heritage provides us with gifts to help us on the journey. Those gifts include our commitment to critical reflection, social justice, and belief in a God who is to be trusted more than feared. When these gifts are enriched by an experiential relationship with God and nourished by the spiritual exercises that have shaped our Protestant heritage, our religious expressions foster an integration of mind and heart, body and spirit, prayer and social action. Claiming our "lived experience of the Protestant faith" allows us to celebrate the gifts we share with those of other traditions, as well as those that emerge from our own particular way of being faithful in the world.

This book provides guidelines for using spiritual disciplines rooted in the Protestant tradition. Those who find their interest piqued by this material may benefit from exploring a wide variety of other resources that are available today. Books and periodicals on prayer and spirituality abound in bookstores and libraries, as well as on the Internet. Our own faith communities may also offer resources and leadership in the area of spiritual development. As mainline Protestant denominations become more aware of importance of spiritual growth, programs are being developed at national, regional, and congregational levels that address this concern. The appendix to this book, while not an exhaustive list of programs, provides some resources for those seeking further guidance on this life-transforming journey.

As we begin to awaken to God's loving call in our lives, many of us start using spiritual disciplines as ways to guide and deepen our relationship with the holy. Conversely, when we are faithful to our spiritual disciplines we increase the possibility of deepening our awareness of God's movement and call on our lives.

That awareness helps us to pray and act as if the quality of our lives depends on our relationship with God. And, of course, it does.

Appendix

TRAINING CENTERS

Academy for Spiritual Formation
The Upper Room
P.O. Box 189
Nashville, TN 37202-0189
USA
615-340-7232

Archdiocese of Louisville
1200 S. Shelby St.
Louisville, KY 40203-2600
USA
Contact: Steve Wirth, Office of Spirituality
Wk: 502-636-0296
Fx: 502-636-2379

Bethel Seminary
5847 Hobe Lane
White Bear Lake, MN 55110
USA

Center for Christian Spirituality
General Theological Seminary of the Episcopal Church
175 Ninth Avenue
New York, NY 10011-4977
USA
Tel: 212-243-5150
Fx: 212-727-3907
Web: www.gts.edu

Center for Religious Development
2240 Massachusetts Avenue
Cambridge, MA 02140
USA
Contact: Fr. Kenneth J. Hughes
Wk: 617-547-4122
Fx: 617-491-9945

Christos Center/Spiritual Formation
1212 Holly Drive West
Lino Lakes, MN 55038-9703
USA
Contact: Joann Nesser
Wk: 612-653-8207

Christos Prayer Center
5023 Edgewater Drive
Mound, MN 55364
USA

Christos Prayer Center
600 Suzanne Avenue
St. Paul, MN 55126
USA

Christos Prayer Center
4244 Elizabeth Lane
Vadnais Heights, MN 55127
USA

Creighton University
2500 California
Omaha, NE 68178
USA
Contact: Renee L. O'Brien
Wk: 402-280-2996
Fx: 402-288-2423

Dayspring Center for Spirituality
28220 Quarry Road
Wellington, OH 44090-9245
USA
Contact: Virginia LeDare Cox
Wk: 419-929-2585
Fx: 419-939-2585

Guelph Centre of Spirituality
Loyola House, Ignatius College
P.O. Box 245
Guelph, ONT
CANADA N1H 6J9
Contact: Sr. Elaine Frigo, CSSF
Wk: 519-824-1250 x254

Institute for Spiritual Leadership
Chicago Theological Seminary
P.O. Box 53147
Chicago, IL 60653-0147
USA
Contact: Sr. Patricia M. Irr, OSF
Wk: 773-752-7953
Fx: 773-752-5964

Mercy Center
SD Training Programs
2300 Adeline Drive
Burlingame, CA 94010
USA
Wk: 650-340-7400
Fx: 650-340-1299

San Francisco Theological Seminary
Certificate in Spiritual Direction
2 Kensington Road
San Anselmo, CA 94960
USA
Contact: Dr. Andrew Dreitcer
Wk: 415-258-6583

School for Charismatic Spiritual Directors
Benedictine Monastery
Pecos, NM 87552
USA
Wk: 505-757-6415 x239
Fx: 505-757-2285

Shalem Institute for Spiritual Formation
530 Grosvenor Lane
Bethesda, MD 20814
USA
Contact: Rose Mary Dougherty, SSND
Wk: 301-897-7334 x107
Fx: 301-897-3719
E-mail: info@shalem.org

Stillpoint
1008-19th Avenue
Nashville, TN 37212-2166
USA
Contact: Rev. Donna Scott
Wk: 615-340-7557
Fx: 615-340-7463
E-mail: spiritsbc@juno.com

Stillpoint/Centerpoint Spiritual Direction Program
P.O. Box 3722
Santa Barbara, CA 93130
USA
Contact: Rev. Martha A. Siegel, D.Min.
Wk: 805-684-5284
Fx: 805-565-3190
E-mail: MBSiegel@west.net

Tacheheria Spirituality Centre
P.O. Box 65840
Tucson, AZ 85728
USA
Contact: Dr. Jeannette L. Renouf
Wk: 520-299-6421 x34
Fx: 520-299-0712

Tatamagouche Centre
Tatamagouche, NS
CANADA BOK 1VO
Contact: Don MacDougall
Wk: 902-657-2231

Notes

INTRODUCTION

[1]Wade Clark Roof and William McKinney, *American Mainline Religion: Its Changing Shape and Future* (New Brunswick, NJ: Rutgers University Press, 1992), pp. 72–105.

[2]Quotation from *Vogue* magazine in Kathleen Norris, *The Cloister Walk* (New York: Riverhead Books, 1996), p. 314.

[3]C. Kirk Hadaway and David A. Roozen, *Rerouting the Protestant Mainstream: Sources of Growth and Opportunities for Change* (Nashville, TN: Abingdon Press, 1995), pp. 73–89.

CHAPTER 1
THEOLOGICAL AFFIRMATIONS

[1]Seward Hiltner, *Self Understanding Through Psychology and Religion* (New York: Scribner's Sons, 1951), p. 122.

[2]Sandra Schneiders, "A Hermeneutical Approach to the Study of Christian Spirituality" *Christian Spirituality Bulletin* (Spring 1994): 9–14.

[3]Roof and McKinney, *American Mainline Religion*, pp. 7–8, 51–51.

[4]Rudolf Otto, *The Idea of the Holy: An Inquiry into the Non-rational in the Idea of the Divine and Its Relation to the Rational* (New York: Oxford University Press, 1958).

[5]Abraham Maslow, *Religion, Values and Peak-experiences* (Columbus: Ohio State University Press, 1964).

[6]William A. Barry, S.J. and William Connolly, *The Practice of Spiritual Direction* (San Francisco: Harper and Row, Publishers, 1982), p. 34.

[7]Robertson Davies, *Fifth Business* (New York: Penguin Books, 1978), pp. 176–177.

[8]Martin Brecht, Martin Luther: *His Road to Reformation 1483–1521* (Minneapolis: Fortress Press, 1993), p. 255.

[9]Philipp Jakob Spener, "From the *Pia Desideria*" in *Pietists: Selected Writings*, ed. by Peter C. Erb, "The Classics of Western Spirituality," (New York: Paulist Press, 1983) 31–49.

CHAPTER 2
THE DEVELOPMENT OF SPIRITUAL LIFE

[1]Teresa of Avila, *The Interior Castle*, trans. Kieran Kavanaugh, O.C.D. and Otilio Rodriguez, O.C.D. "The Classics of Western Spirituality," (New York: Paulist Press, 1979).

[2]Ibid., 7, 4, 9.

[3]James Finley, Lecture, Sisters of St. Joseph Mother House, London, Ontario. Spring, 1979. Further development of this will appear in James Finley, *The Seeker's Heart: Explorations in Contemplative Living* (Notre Dame: Ave Marie Press, 1999).

[4]The three circles of this model were developed in the late 1970s in workshops by August Meacham and R. Maurice Boyd. I have expanded their original work to provide for spiritual exercises.

[5]August Meacham, personal correspondence, November 1997.

[6]John H. Mostyn, CFC. Workshop: Certificate in the Art of Spiritual Direction, Supervision Training, Program in Christian Spirituality, San Francisco Theological Seminary, San Anselmo California, March 15–16, 1996.

[7]Jonathan Edwards, "Personal Narrative" from *The Works of President Edwards*, ed. Samuel Austin, 8 vols. (Worcester, MA: 1808–09), 1:34–44.

[8]Barbel Inhelder and Jean Piaget, *The Growth of Logical Thinking from Childhood to Adolescence* (New York: Basis Books, 1958). James W. Fowler, *Stages of Faith: The Psychology of Human Development and the Quest for Meaning* (San Francisco: Harper and Row, 1981). Lawrence Kohlberg, *The Psychology of Moral Development: The Nature and Validity of Moral Stages* (San Francisco: Harper and Row, 1984). Jane Loevinger, *Ego Development* (San Francisco: Jossey-Bass Publishers, 1976).

[9]Elizabeth Liebert, *Charging Life Patterns: Adult Development in Spiritual Direction* (New York: Paulist Press, 1992). Mary Bray Pipher, *Reviving Ophelia: Saving the Selves of Adolescent Girls* (New York: Putnam, 1994). Carol Gilligan, *In A Different Voice: Psychological Theory and Women's Development* (Cambridge: Harvard University Press, 1982).

CHAPTER 3
GUIDELINES FOR USING SPIRITUAL PRACTICES

[1]Kathleen Battle, Jessye Norman. Compact Disc. "Spirituals in Concert." Deutsche Grammophon, No. 297902, 1991.

CHAPTER 4
SPIRITUAL PRACTICES

[1]Herbert Benson, *The Relaxation Response* (New York: William Morrow, 1975). Progressive deep muscle relaxation was first developed by Edmund Jackson, *Progressive Relaxation* (Chicago: University of Chicago Press, 1938).

[2]Monastic communities continue to exist within the Anglican Communion but they generally follow Rules established prior to the Reformation, for example, The Rule of Benedict.

[3]*Chalice Worship*, ed. Colbert S. Cartwright and O.I. Cricket Harrison. St. Louis, MO: Chalice Press, 1997.

[4]Brecht, *Luther*, p. 200.

[5]Martin Luther, *A Simple Way to Pray*, trans. Carl J. Schindler, in *Luther's Works*, vol. 43, Devotional Writings II, ed. Gustav K. Wiencke (Philadelphia Fortress Press, 1968): 187–211.

[6]John Calvin, *The Institutes of the Christian Religion*, ed. John T. McNeill, trans. Ford Lewis Battles, (Philadelphia: Westminster Press, 1960), Book III, XX, iii, p. 852.

[7]Ibid., Chapter XX, iv–xiv, pp. 853–870, contain the four rules and the phrases quoted.

[8]Ibid., Chapter XI, Article x, p. 737.

[9]I have used the prayer form of Earle and Elspeth Williams, *Spiritually Aware Pastoral Care: An Introduction and Training Program*, (New York: Paulist Press, 1992), p. 127, and rewritten sections to focus explicitly on actions in daily life.

[10]C.W. Dugmore, "Canonical Hours," in The Westminster Dictionary of Worship, 1972.

[11]*American Heritage Dictionary of the English Language*.

[12]Ira Progoff, *At a Journal Workshop: The Basic Text and Guide for Using the Intensive Journal Process* (New York: Dialogue House Library, 1975).

[13]This follows the structure of covenants in David Lowes Watson, *Accountable Discipleship: Handbook for Covenant Disciples Groups in the Congregation* (Nashville: Discipleship Resources, 1986), pp. 64–66.

Bibliography

Cobb, John B. *Praying for Jennifer: An Exploration of Intercessory Prayer in Story Form.* Nashville: Upper Room, 1985.
 Friends of Jennifer, a comatose teenager injured in an automobile accident, form a prayer group to pray for her. Their prayers and discussions open up the topic of intercessory prayer. Helpful for groups and individuals struggling to understand how God heals through prayer.

Dupré, Louis and Don E. Salliers, eds. *Christian Spirituality: Post-Reformation and Modern.* New York: Crossroad, 1989.
 Essays on Protestant and Roman Catholic schools and movements of the post-Reformation and Modern periods include the spiritual expressions associated with Pietism, Anglicanism, Puritanism and Pentecostalism. The spirituality of African-American traditions and the spirituality of the Christian feminist movement are explored in addition to those of sixteenth- to eighteenth-century Roman Catholic movements.

Edwards, Jonathan. *The Religious Affections.* Carlisle, Pennsylvania: The Banner of Truth Trust, 1994.
 For, among others, United Church of Christ members with an interest in history and spiritual guidance. Jonathan Edwards' treatment of "distinguishing signs of truly gracious and holy affections," as well as signs that offer no certainty, are as valuable today as they were in 1746 when first published.

Erb, Peter C., ed. *Pietists: Selected Writings.* New York: Paulist Press, 1983.
 A helpful introduction presents selections from the primary works of a number of pietists. Considerable attention is paid to Spener, Franck and the Halle School. Those interested in spirituality today from a Protestant vantage point will be well served by familiarity with these historical documents.

Farrington, Debra. *Romancing the Holy.* New York: The Crossroad Publishing Company, 1997.
Provides an accessible and informative introduction to spiritual direction, retreats, prayer groups and even "online" spirituality. This is an excellent resource for those inside and those outside the church who want to know more about spiritual practices.

Foster, Richard J. and Kathryn A. Yanni. *Celebrating the Disciplines: A Journal Workbook to Accompany Celebration of Discipline.* San Francisco: Harper, 1992.
Workbook that builds on Foster's earlier *Celebration of Discipline.* Provides an introduction to a number of spiritual practices associated with inward (e.g., prayer), outward (e.g., service) and corporate (e.g., worship) disciplines.

Jones, Alan. *Journey into Christ.* Cambridge, Massachusetts: Cowley Publications, 1992.
Pilgrimage and journey, darkness and light, myth and symbol, transcendence and transfiguration are the stuff of this work by the Dean of Grace Cathedral. This theological reflection on the nature of spiritual pilgrimage invites us—with due warning—to make the journey into Christ.

Keating, Thomas. *Invitation to Love: The Way of Christian Contemplation.* New York: Continuum, 1995.
This work provides guidance for using centering prayer as a regular spiritual discipline. Keating explores the nature of the healing that occurs when one deepens one's relationship with God. Chapters include: "The False Self in Action," "From Contemplation to Action," and "Spirituality in Everyday Life."

Klug, Ronald. *How to Keep a Spiritual Journal: A Guide to Journal Keeping for Inner Growth and Personal Discovery.* Minneapolis: Augsburg, 1993.
Practical guide that explores the significance, role, and purpose of journal keeping. Helpful to anyone who wishes to explore journal keeping as a spiritual discipline.

Leech, Kenneth. *True Prayer: An Invitation to Christian Spirituality.* Harrisburg, Pennsylvania: Morehouse Publishing, 1980.

Leech, an Anglican priest, has spent much of his ministry in London's East End working on issues of spirituality, ministry, and social and economic justice. This work addresses the understanding of prayer that informs his spiritual life and sustains his vision. It provides a meaningful theology of prayer.

Liebert, Elizabeth, SNJM. *Changing Life Patterns: Adult Development in Spiritual Direction.* New York: Paulist Press, 1992. This volume builds on the work of a number of ego development theorists, including Jane Loevinger and Robert Keagan, to explore the contribution psychological theory can make to spiritual development. Case studies of two women and two men seeking spiritual direction are effectively used to illuminate the theoretical material.

Maas, Robin and Gabriel O'Donnell, O.P. *Spiritual Traditions for the Contemporary Church.* Nashville: Abingdon Press, 1990. An ecumenical historical survey of major Christian spiritual traditions. Theoretical/historical material is followed throughout with a chapter on experiential practices. This resource will be especially useful to those interested in both theory and practice.

McGinn, Bernard and John Meyendorff, eds. *Christian Spirituality: Origins to the Twelfth Century.* New York: Crossroad, 1987. This work provides essays on the periods, movements, themes, and values that shaped the early period of Christian spirituality. Helpful bibliographies are provided with each of the nineteen major issues. Topics include: "Scripture and Spirituality," "Spirituality in Celtic and Germanic Society," "Icon and Art," and "Ways of Prayer and Contemplation."

Paulsell, William O. *Taste and See: A Personal Guide to the Spiritual Life.* St. Louis: Chalice Press, 1992. Accessible guide for people or groups seeking an introduction to spiritual development. Paulsell is a Christian Church (Disciples in Christ) pastor and former president of Lexington Theological Seminary. Chapters include: Beginning, Silence, Meditation, and Prayer.

Raitt, Jill, ed. *Christian Spirituality: High Middle Ages and Reformation*. New York: Crossroad Publishing Company, 1988. Noted scholars provide essays in this historical survey of major figures, movements, and themes. Movements include Dominican, Franciscan, Carmelite, and Augustinian spiritualities; figures include Luther, Calvin, and Zwingli. A closing essay explores Roman Catholic and Protestant spirituality in the sixteenth century.

Rice, Howard. *Reformed Spirituality: An Introduction for Believers*. Louisville, Kentucky: Westminster/John Knox Press, 1991. This work provides an accessible overview of Reformed spirituality that will be especially useful to Presbyterians and United Church of Christ members. Given the breadth of Calvin's influence, other Protestant groups will also find this rewarding.

Sadler, Kim Martin, ed. *The Book of Daily Prayer*. Cleveland, Ohio: United Church Press, 1996. Prayers and readings for morning and evening devotions for each day of 1997 are provided by a variety of pastors, administrators, and academics primarily but not exclusively from the United Church of Christ.

Senn, Frank C. *Protestant Spiritual Traditions*. New York: Paulist Press, 1986. A brief historical overview of a number of Protestant spiritual traditions: Lutheran, Reformed, Anabaptist, Anglican, Puritan, Pietist, and Methodist. This work highlights the context from which the variety of Protestant spiritual traditions emerged.

Thompson, Marjorie J. *Soul Feast: An Invitation to the Christian Spiritual Life*. Louisville, Kentucky: Westminster John Knox Press, 1995. Individuals, small groups, and congregations will find nurture for their spirits in this introduction and guide to the spiritual life. This resource considers such topics as prayer, worship, fasting, hospitality, spiritual direction, and many others with an eye to developing spiritual practices and creating a rule of life.

Thurman, Howard. *With Head and Heart.* San Diego: Harcourt
Brace Jovanovich, Publishers, 1979.
   A stunning autobiography of one of America's greatest religious leaders. Thurman's reflections on his experiences as
   an African-American leader in the U.S. expose not only the
   depth of his spirituality, but also the forces of racism and
   oppression with which he had to contend.

Wesley, John and Charles. *Selected Prayers, Hymns, Journal Notes,
Sermons, Letters and Treatises.* Edited with an introduction by
Frank Whaling. *The Classics of Western Spirituality* series. New
York: Paulist Press, 1981.
   A helpful introduction to a variety of selections from pri-
   mary works by John and Charles Wesley. Useful background
   for understanding Methodist spirituality.

Washington, James Melvin. *Conversations with God: Two Centuries of Prayers by African Americans.* San Francisco: Harper
Collins Publishers, 1994.
   An anthology of prayers from a "determined yet degraded
   people" (Cornel West). Through these works one enters a
   rich depth of African-American spirituality.

Wicks, Robert J. *Handbook of Spirituality for Ministers.* New
York: Paulist Press, 1995.
   This is a wonderful resource for clergy who are seeking to
   integrate increased spiritual depth into their ministerial
   practices. Thirty-five short essays address such issues as
   spiritual guidance, prayer, social justice, the spirituality of
   the minister, ministering to Hispanics, African-American
   spirituality, psychology, and spiritual guidance.

Wuellner, Flora Slosson. *Feed My Shepherds: Spiritual Healing
and Renewal for Those in Christian Leadership.* Nashville: Upper
Room Books, 1998.
   Explores the issues of burnout, fatigue, the internalization
   of others' needs, and other self-care issues that affect clergy,
   spiritual directors, and others who exercise Christian leadership in these ways. Through scriptural stories, guided
   meditations, and reflection questions, Wuellner helps leaders care for themselves as they care for others.